General Knowledge Crosswords

Phil Clarke

Illustrated by the Pope Twins

Designed by Michael Hill

Edited by Sam Taplin

How to solve crosswords

The crosswords in this book start simple and gradually get harder. If you're new to crosswords, here are a few tips.

It's a good idea to use a pencil with an eraser or to write lightly with a pen so that you can remove or write over mistakes.

There are two lists of clues: one for answers that read across the crossword grid, and one for those that read down.

Start wherever you like. If you can't solve one clue, move onto another that crosses it. The letters from that answer will help you. For example, solving the across answers below gives you C_R_O for 2 down, leading you towards the answer: CARGO.

ACROSS

1. Parent's brother (5)
3. It's fired with a bow (5)
5. Red liquid in your veins (5)

DOWN

1. America (1.1.1.)
2. Ship's goods (5)
4. Marry (3)

After each clue you can see how many letters the answer has, and whether it contains one word or more.

If you get stuck, or your words don't seem to fit, you can check all the answers at the back of the book.

Happy puzzling!

1

Puzzle 1 grid:

¹F	o	²a	l	
a		l		³j
⁴c	h	i	c	k
t		v		i
⁵s	l	e	e	p

ACROSS
1. Baby horse (4)
4. Baby bird (5)
5. Rest, slumber (5)

DOWN
1. Pieces of information (5)
2. Living (5)
3. Hop, bound (4)

2

Puzzle 2 grid:

	¹l	a	²m	³b
⁴c		r		u
⁵a	n	g	r	y
d		u		s
⁶f	r	e	t	

ACROSS
1. Baby sheep (4)
5. Annoyed (5)
6. Worry (4)

DOWN
2. Disagree, fight (5)
3. Purchases (4)
4. Baby cow (4)

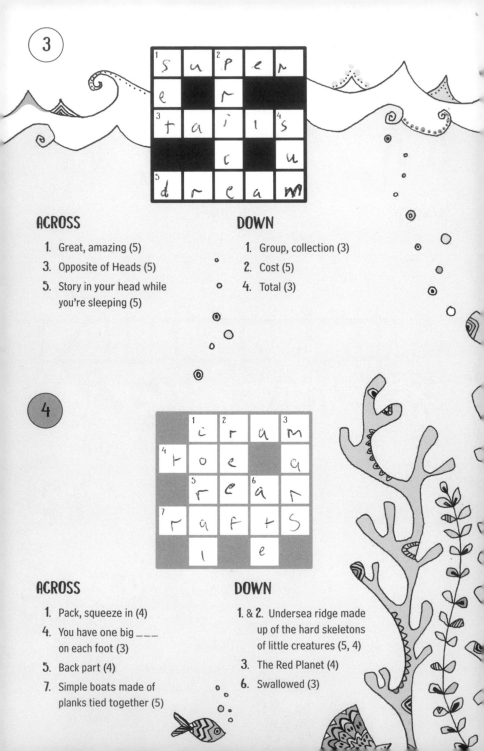

3

Grid (completed):
Row 1: S U . P E R
Row 2: E . R . .
Row 3: T A I L S
Row 4: . . C . U
Row 5: D R E A M

ACROSS

1. Great, amazing (5)
3. Opposite of Heads (5)
5. Story in your head while you're sleeping (5)

DOWN

1. Group, collection (3)
2. Cost (5)
4. Total (3)

4

Grid (completed):
Row 1: C R A M
Row 2: T O E . Q
Row 3: R E A R
Row 4: R A F T S
Row 5: L . E

ACROSS

1. Pack, squeeze in (4)
4. You have one big ___ on each foot (3)
5. Back part (4)
7. Simple boats made of planks tied together (5)

DOWN

1. & 2. Undersea ridge made up of the hard skeletons of little creatures (5, 4)
3. The Red Planet (4)
6. Swallowed (3)

Puzzle 5 grid (filled):

f	i		s	h
o		c	a	p
a	l	a	s	
m	a	n	t	a
	w		e	

ACROSS

1. Finned water creature (4)
4. Peaked hat (3)
5. Old-fashioned word used to express sorrow (4)
7. _____ ray, huge flat fish with wing-like fins (5)

DOWN

1. Froth (4)
2. Medical image (4)
3. Hurried, careless (5)
6. Rule (3)

Puzzle 6 grid (filled):

c	a	t		e
o		h		u
c	l	o	w	n
o		r		n
a	n	n	o	y

ACROSS

1. Purring pet (3)
4. Funny circus entertainer (5)
5. Bother, irritate (5)

DOWN

1. Main ingredient of hot chocolate (5)
2. Large prickle on a plant (5)
3. Comical (5)

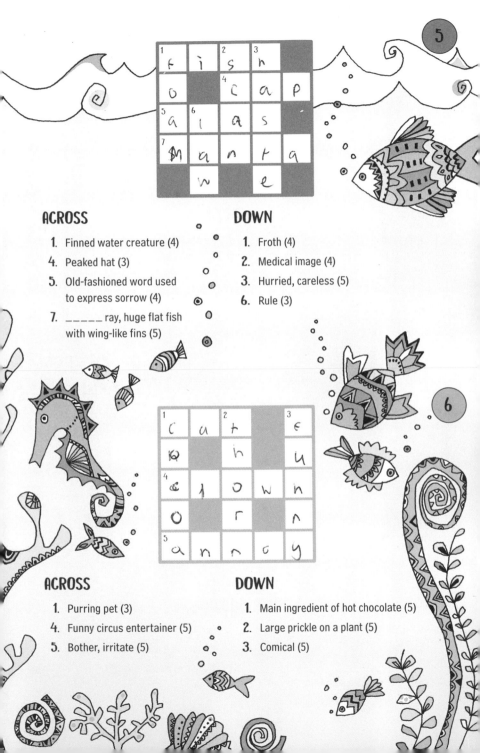

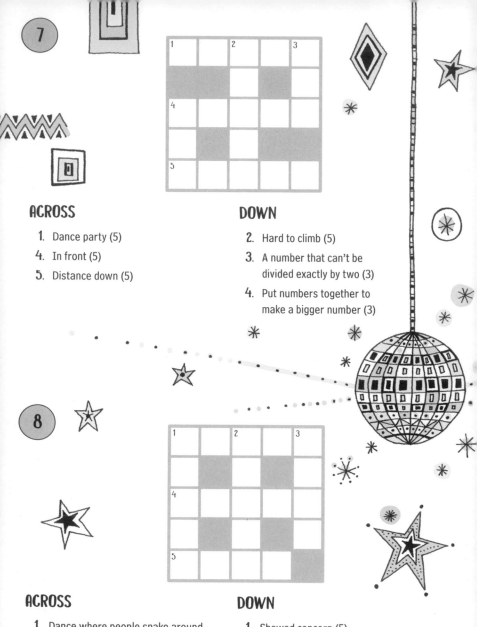

7

ACROSS

1. Dance party (5)
4. In front (5)
5. Distance down (5)

DOWN

2. Hard to climb (5)
3. A number that can't be divided exactly by two (3)
4. Put numbers together to make a bigger number (3)

8

ACROSS

1. Dance where people snake around the room in a long line (5)
4. Lift up (5)
5. What the "D" in DJ stands for (4)

DOWN

1. Showed concern (5)
2. You hit them with a hammer (5)
3. Long stretches of time (4)

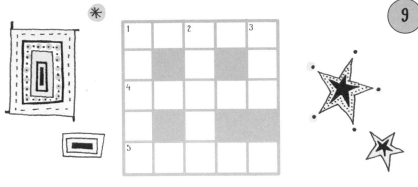

ACROSS

1. Turn your upper body (5)
4. Clean the floor with a broom (5)
5. Latin American dance, or a chunky dipping sauce (5)

DOWN

1. An elephant's largest teeth (5)
2. Perfect (5)
3. Noisy dance in metal-soled shoes (3)

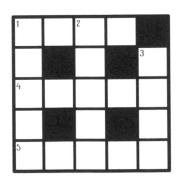

ACROSS

1. Dice shape (4)
4. Conscious, knowing (5)
5. Twitter message (5)

DOWN

1. List of the week's most popular songs (5)
2. Burn brightly (5)
3. Pulse, rhythm (4)

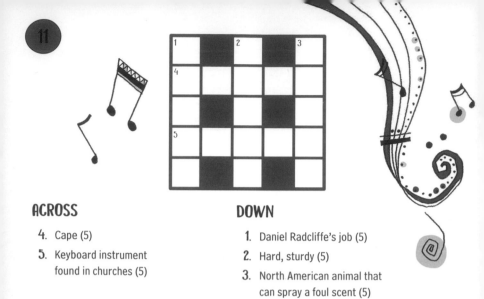

11

ACROSS

4. Cape (5)
5. Keyboard instrument found in churches (5)

DOWN

1. Daniel Radcliffe's job (5)
2. Hard, sturdy (5)
3. North American animal that can spray a foul scent (5)

12

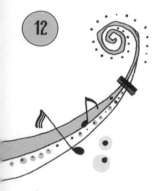
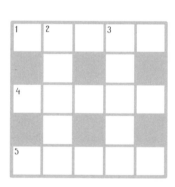

ACROSS

1. Range of musical notes increasing in pitch (5)
4. Woodwind instrument (5)
5. Entrances (5)

DOWN

2. Instrument like a large violin, played sitting down (5)
3. Afterwards (5)

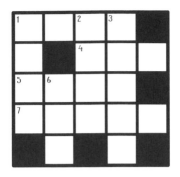

ACROSS

1. Telephone conversation (4)
4. You use it for hearing (3)
5. Missing (4)
7. Rock or classical, for example (5)

DOWN

1. Peaceful (4)
2. Not as much (4)
3. Language of Ancient Rome (5)
6. Not at home (3)

ACROSS

1. Keyboard instrument (5)
4. Bag_____, Scottish musical instrument (5)
5. There are 52 in a year (5)

DOWN

1. Short for popular music (3)
2. More than enough (5)
3. Green area around a pool in the desert (5)

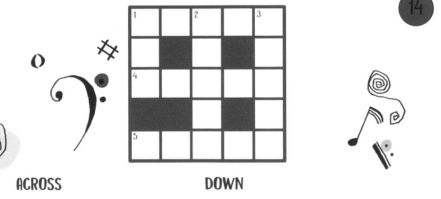

15

ACROSS

1. Oxygen, for example (3)
4. Hole, ditch (3)
5. Distant (3)
6. Used to start a car (3)

DOWN

1. Sport where you swing a club (4)
2. It lights the fuel in an engine (5)
3. Boot-shaped country in the Mediterranean Sea (5)

16

ACROSS

1. Steering _ _ _ _ _ (5)
4. Henry the Eighth's last name (5)
5. Drivers honk this to let other people know they're there (4)

DOWN

1. Wrist clock (5)
2. Person older than you (5)
3. Lie in wait (4)

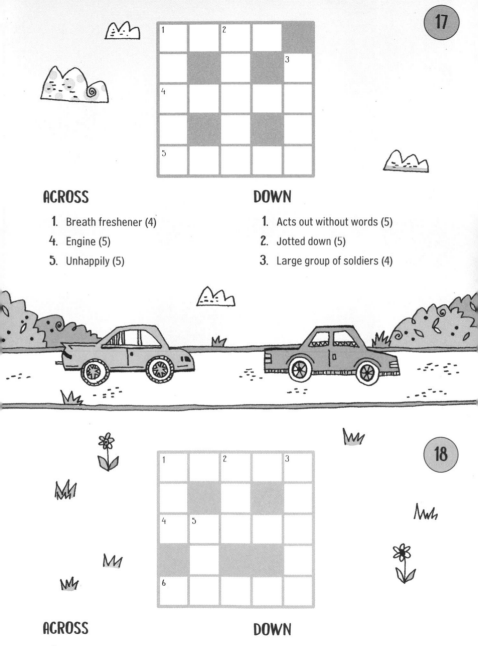

ACROSS

1. Breath freshener (4)
4. Engine (5)
5. Unhappily (5)

DOWN

1. Acts out without words (5)
2. Jotted down (5)
3. Large group of soldiers (4)

ACROSS

1. Sadness after someone has died (5)
4. Guide a vehicle (5)
6. Concentrate (5)

DOWN

1. Car navigation computer (1.1.1.)
2. ___ cubes, used to cool drinks (3)
3. They go with knives (5)
5. Number of wheels on a motorcycle (3)

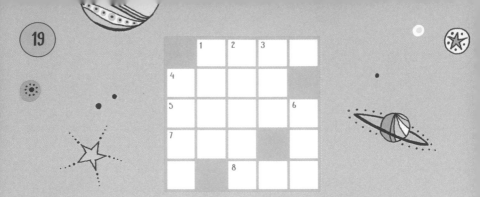

ACROSS

1. Call out in pain or despair (4)
4. Lemons have this kind of taste (4)
5. Musical symbols (5)
7. The first number (3)
8. Sprint (3)

DOWN

1. It circles around the Earth (4)
2. Jupiter, Saturn, Uranus and Neptune are known as the _ _ _ _ _ Planets (5)
3. "I am going; they _ _ _ coming too." (3)
4. It falls in winter (4)
6. The star nearest Earth (3)

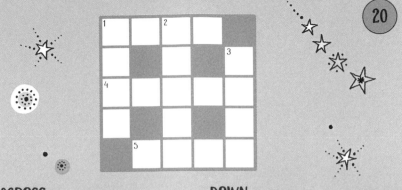

ACROSS

1. Speed contest (4)
4. Bright light with a tail that moves slowly across the sky (5)
5. Healed wound (4)

DOWN

1. Wealthy (4)
2. Magazine with picture stories (5)
3. Blazing ball of gas in space (4)

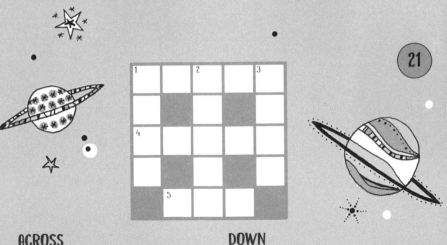

ACROSS

1. To do with the Moon (5)
4. Bright planet named after the Roman goddess of 1 down (5)
5. Farewell (3)

DOWN

1. Strong affection (4)
2. Full-time babysitter (5)
3. Move upwards (4)

22

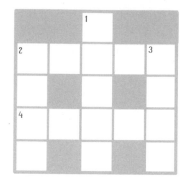

ACROSS

2. Quick, or a swallow-like bird (5)
4. Stadium (5)

DOWN

1. Toys on strings that fly in the wind (5)
2. Large, white water bird (4)
3. Defrost (4)

23

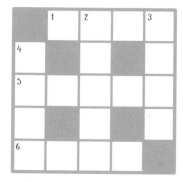

ACROSS

1. Little picture you click to open an app (4)
5. Not asleep (5)
6. Was aware (4)

DOWN

2. Giant lifting vehicle, or a large bird (5)
3. Another word for Christmas, or a boy's name (4)
4. Songbird (4)

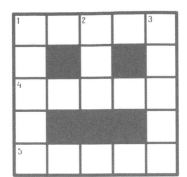

ACROSS

1. Large parrot (5)
4. Red-breasted bird (5)
5. Large bird of prey with a big, hooked beak (5)

DOWN

1. Code made up of dots and dashes (5)
2. Corn on the ___ (3)
3. Grimace, flinch (5)

25

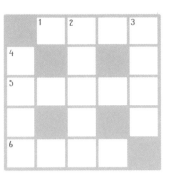

ACROSS

1. Guessing game often played in cars (1-3)
5. Ancient Egyptian corpse preserved in bandages (5)
6. Where you wash your hands (4)

DOWN

2. _ _ _ _ _ Says, follow-the-leader type game (5)
3. Toy on a string (2-2)
4. Short for Christmas (4)

26

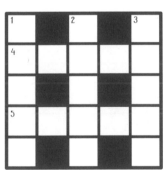

ACROSS

4. Game played on a checkered board (5)
5. Swindler, rascal (5)

DOWN

1. Points won in a game (5)
2. The noise a horse makes (5)
3. Great Britain and Ireland are known together as the British _ _ _ _ _ (5)

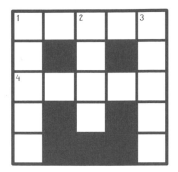

ACROSS

1. Card game, or iron fire tool (5)
4. Willy _____, character in *Charlie and the Chocolate Factory* (5)

DOWN

1. In chess, the least valuable pieces (5)
2. The most important chesspiece (4)
3. Prepared (5)

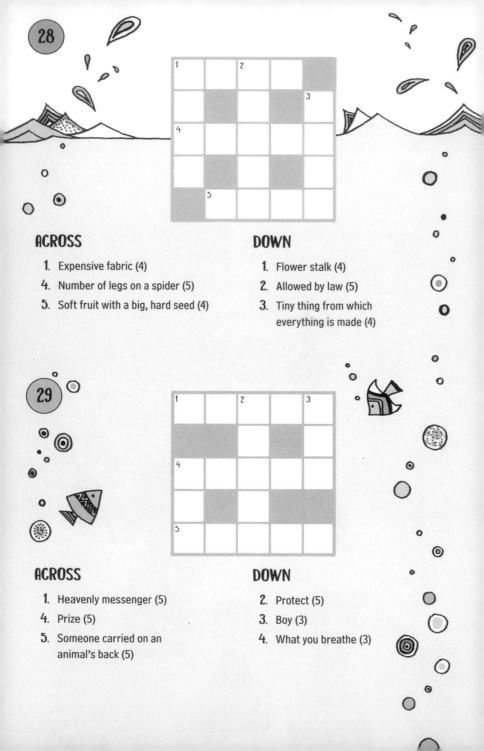

28

ACROSS

1. Expensive fabric (4)
4. Number of legs on a spider (5)
5. Soft fruit with a big, hard seed (4)

DOWN

1. Flower stalk (4)
2. Allowed by law (5)
3. Tiny thing from which everything is made (4)

29

ACROSS

1. Heavenly messenger (5)
4. Prize (5)
5. Someone carried on an animal's back (5)

DOWN

2. Protect (5)
3. Boy (3)
4. What you breathe (3)

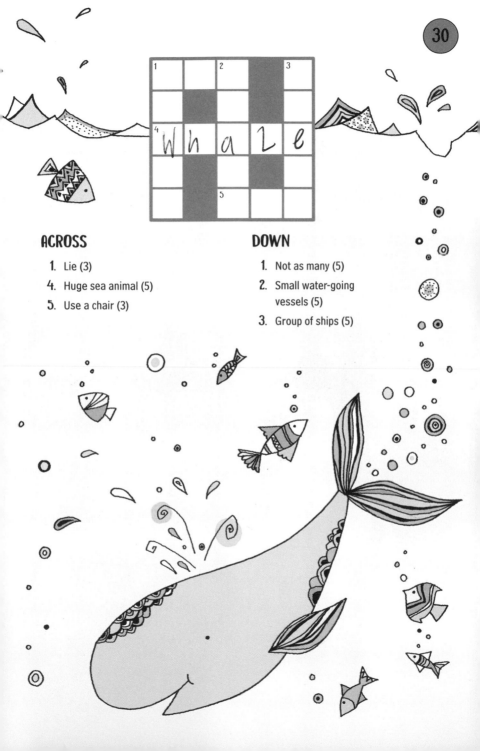

ACROSS

1. Lie (3)
4. Huge sea animal (5)
5. Use a chair (3)

DOWN

1. Not as many (5)
2. Small water-going vessels (5)
3. Group of ships (5)

31

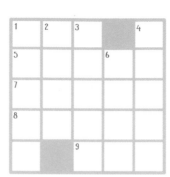

ACROSS

1. The noise a crow makes (3)
5. Out of the way (5)
7. Underground worker (5)
8. Keen (5)
9. Secret agent (3)

DOWN

1. Humped animal (5)
2. The largest continent (4)
3. What a bird uses to fly (5)
4. Very small, round fruit (5)
6. Reaching a long way down (4)

32

ACROSS

1. Coffee mixed with chocolate (5)
4. Middle-eastern meat dish grilled on a spit or skewer (5)
5. Shelter from the sun (5)

DOWN

1. Creates (5)
2. Hooded snake; some types can spit venom (5)
3. Walk at a relaxed pace (5)

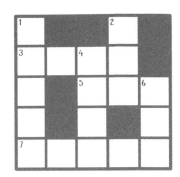

ACROSS

3. White grain often eaten with Asian food (4)
5. Night bird (3)
7. Delicious (5)

DOWN

1. Lara _ _ _ _ _, action-heroine of *Tomb Raider* (5)
2. Fresh (3)
4. Farm animals (4)
6. Put something in place (3)

ACROSS

1. Two Asian countries, North and South _ _ _ _ _, that used to be one (5)
4. Asian country famous for its Great Wall (5)
5. Dropped below the surface (4)

DOWN

1. Strikes with the foot (5)
2. The length of time for which a king or queen rules (5)
3. A slightly open door is _ _ _ _ (4)

35

ACROSS
3. Rabbits love this orange vegetable (6)
5. One with four leaves is lucky (6)
6. Frightens (6)

DOWN
1. Vegetable that scares vampires (6)
2. They bring thunder and lightning (6)
4. Large stream (5)

36

ACROSS
1. Hot-tasting white and pink root vegetable (6)
4. Change direction (4)
6. Pod vegetable, for example kidney _ _ _ _ (4)
7. Stinging green weed (6)

DOWN
1. Cloth strip (6)
2. Computer information (4)
3. What you hold something by (6)
5. Single thing (4)

37

ACROSS

1. Walking up and down (6)
4. Spud (6)
5. Deserved, worked for (6)

DOWN

1. Usually offered along with salt (6)
2. More adorable (5)
3. Pale brown spice (6)

38

ACROSS

4. Entertained (6)
5. White root vegetable (6)
6. The street where Big Bird lives (6)

DOWN

1. Prickly desert plant (6)
2. Defenders, protectors (6)
3. Between small and large (6)

ACROSS

1. An arrow-holder, or to tremble (6)
4. Someone who uses a bow and arrow (6)
5. Forced into place (6)

DOWN

1. Place where rocks and stones are taken out of the earth (6)
2. Pay, earnings (6)
3. Twenty minus nine (6)

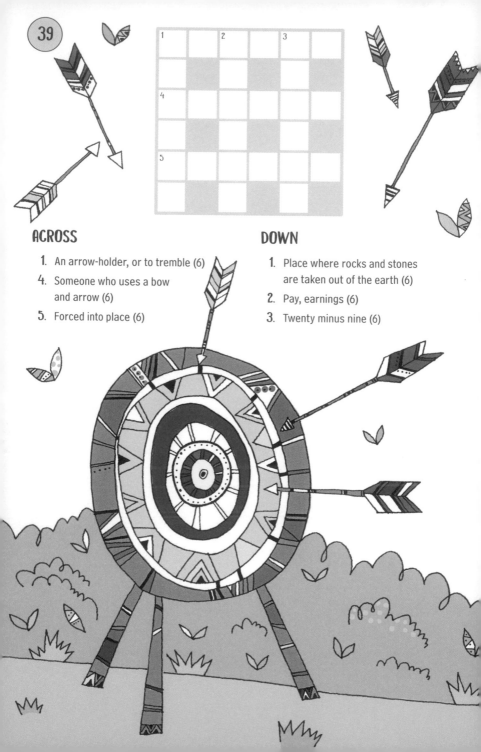

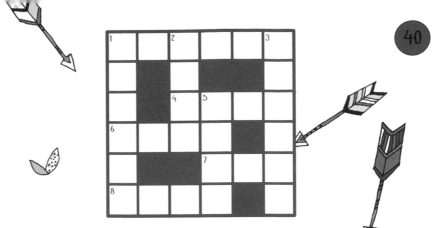

ACROSS

1. Katniss Everdeen wields a bow in The _____ Games (6)
4. Stair (4)
6. Make your choice in an election (4)
7. Top, cover (3)
8. Dirt, earth (4)

DOWN

1. The hard parts of horses' feet (6)
2. Where a bird lays its eggs (4)
3. Violent, fast-flowing part of a river (6)
5. Utter, make known (4)

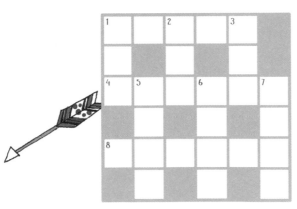

ACROSS

1. (with 7 down) Legendary outlaw who lived in Sherwood Forest (5, 4)
4. Heat (6)
8. Juicy, red salad vegetable (6)

DOWN

1. Line, sequence (3)
2. Iron rod (3)
3. An almond, for example (3)
5. How sailors used to say hello (4)
6. Unkind or stingy (4)
7. (see 1 across)

42

ACROSS

1. Damp (3)
3. Dark green climbing plant (3)
5. Land ruled by royalty (7)
6. Lava-spitting mountain (7)
8. Thick bundle or roll (3)
9. Hang out to dry (3)

DOWN

1. Deep Chinese frying pan (3)
2. Knotted, mixed up (7)
3. Nickname of Henry Jones, movie archaeologist and adventurer (7)
4. " ___! That's delicious." (3)
6. Promise, oath (3)
7. Paddle for a boat (3)

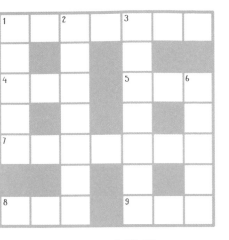

43

ACROSS

1. Tenth month (7)
4. ___-whiz! (3)
5. ___ Hanks, US actor, starred in *Big* and *Turner & Hooch* (3)
7. Child that is starting to walk (7)
8. Fifth month (3)
9. The heavens above (3)

DOWN

1. What you _ _ _ _ _ to do is what you should do. (5)
2. Second day of the working week (7)
3. Wars, conflicts (7)
6. Jolly, happy (5)

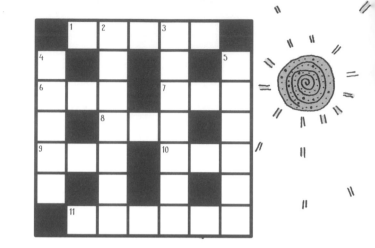

44

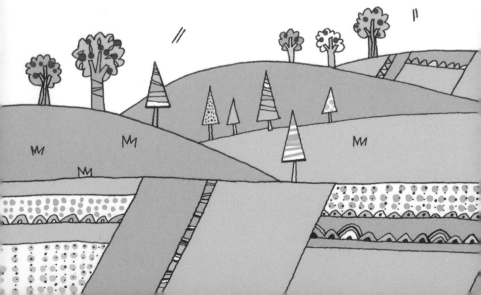

ACROSS

1. Teddy-bear-like Australian animal that lives in trees (5)
6. Small insect that lives in a large group (3)
7. Lip, edge (3)
8. Sack, holdall (3)
9. Long period of time (3)
10. Ostrich-like Australian bird (3)
11. Rough drawing (6)

DOWN

2. The Australian wilderness (7)
3. Biggest (7)
4. They go up and down on the surface of the sea (5)
5. Surprise attack (6)

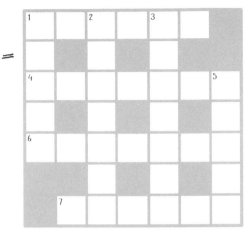

ACROSS

1. Torn (6)
4. Two-wheeled vehicle with pedals (7)
6. Farm vehicle (7)
7. Person in charge (6)

DOWN

1. Android, mechanical person (5)
2. Wrapped item of mail (7)
3. Thrilled (7)
5. Mistake (5)

ACROSS

1. Sea raiders (7)
4. "We took some bread and ___ the ducks." (3)
6. Black, sticky stuff used on roads (3)
8. High-pitched bark (3)
10. The skull-and-crossbones flag used by 1 across was known as the "Jolly _____." (5)
12. Pull another vehicle (3)

DOWN

1. Seaside town (4)
2. How 1 across used to say "yes" (3)
3. You use this to clean your hands (4)
4. "They wandered to and ___." (3)
5. Liquid used to tint hair or clothing (3)
7. Paintings, sculptures, etc. (3)
9. Upper limb (3)
11. Slime (3)

ACROSS

1. Large country north of the USA (6)
4. Hinted at (7)
7. Country between France and the Netherlands (7)
9. Plates, bowls (6)

DOWN

1. Ascend, scale (5)
2. Small country in the Himalayas (5)
3. How old you are (3)
5. Nationality of U2's lead singer, Bono (5)
6. Drops roughly in a heap (5)
8. Finish (3)

ACROSS

5. The period following the Bronze Age (4, 3)
6. Castle jail (7)
7. Water protecting a castle (4)
8. Battering ___, weapon used to attack castles (3)

DOWN

1. Last name of the British royal family (7)
2. Heap, small hill (5)
3. King Arthur's castle (7)
4. Nuts that are often salted (7)

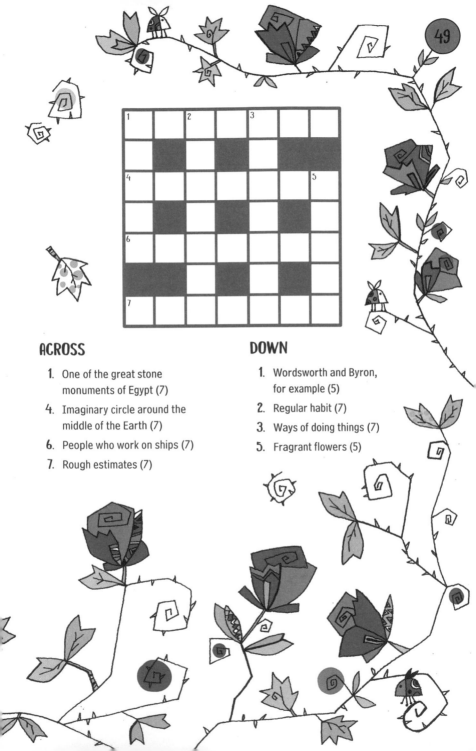

49

ACROSS

1. One of the great stone monuments of Egypt (7)
4. Imaginary circle around the middle of the Earth (7)
6. People who work on ships (7)
7. Rough estimates (7)

DOWN

1. Wordsworth and Byron, for example (5)
2. Regular habit (7)
3. Ways of doing things (7)
5. Fragrant flowers (5)

50

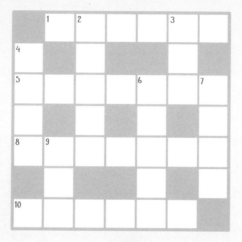

ACROSS

1. Logo, emblem (6)
5. Bank _ _ _ _ _ _ _ , where you can keep your money (7)
8. Countries (7)
10. Women's clothes worn on the lower body (6)

DOWN

2. Boat with a tricky spelling (5)
3. Possess (3)
4. Farm building (4)
6. German submarine used in the World Wars (1-4)
7. Exam (4)
9. Noah's big boat (3)

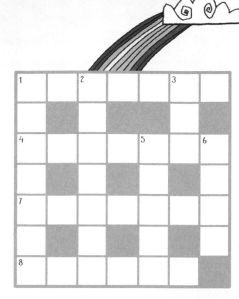

ACROSS

1. A region's typical weather (7)
4. You might find a pot of gold at the end of this (7)
7. Cream-filled French pastries with chocolate on top (7)
8. Threw (6)

DOWN

1. A flow of water or air (7)
2. Frozen drips (7)
3. Number of singers in a duet (3)
5. A woman on her wedding day (5)
6. Clean yourself (4)

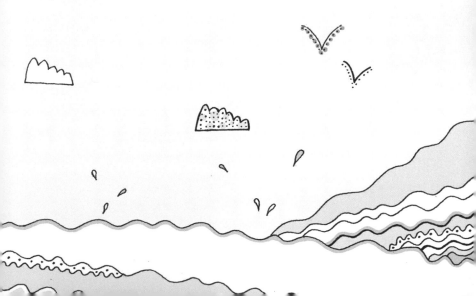

52

ACROSS

1. Small fruits growing on vines (6)
5. Ship that sank when it hit an iceberg in 1912 (7)
6. _____ Jackson, the "King of Pop", who died in 2009 (7)
9. Four-sided shape (6)

DOWN

2. Dried 1 across (7)
3. *James and the Giant* _____ (5)
4. Grin (5)
7. Cry of triumph or surprise (3)
8. Not tell the truth (3)

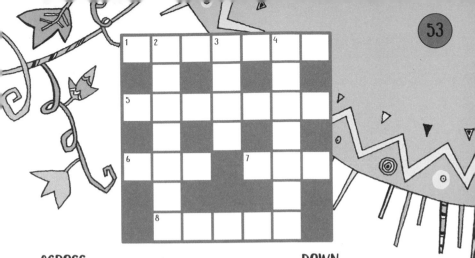

53

ACROSS

1. Japanese art of paper-folding (7)
5. Medieval Japanese warriors (7)
6. The Japanese flag is white and ___. (3)
7. Japan is known as the Land of the Rising ___ (3)
8. Let others use your things (5)

DOWN

2. Book users (7)
3. Sad, moody (4)
4. Find out the length (7)

54

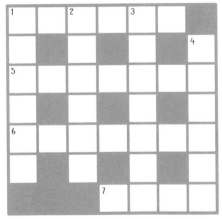

ACROSS

1. On land (6)
5. Mythical creature, half-man, half-horse (7)
6. Say what will happen in the future (7)
7. Place where fresh water is drawn up from the ground (4)

DOWN

1. Receive (6)
2. A boy in a fairy tale who finds a gingerbread house in the woods with his sister (6)
3. Understand (7)
4. 2 down's sister (6)

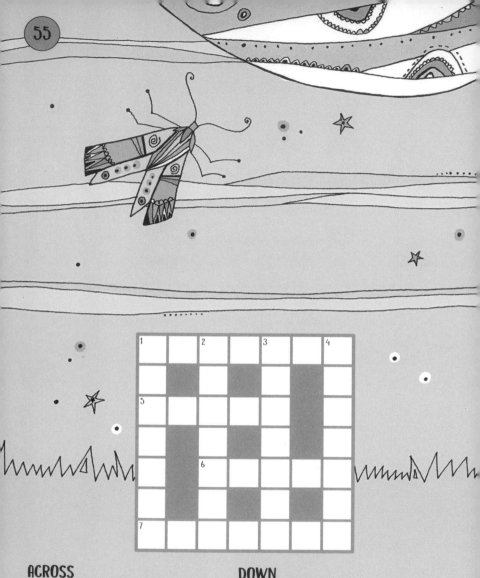

ACROSS

1. King of England, nicknamed the Lionheart (7)
5. The first Emperor of all Russia, known as "the Great" (5)
6. The eighth English king of this name is famous for his six wives (5)
7. Dangle (7)

DOWN

1. Says again (7)
2. Captures (7)
3. Organize (7)
4. Late, held up (7)

ACROSS

1. Wishes (5)
5. Common working person in the Middle Ages (7)
6. Legendary tribe of female warriors (7)
7. People entertaining guests (5)

DOWN

2. Ancient Egyptian ruler (7)
3. Dark shapes that form where light is blocked (7)
4. Night insects that are attracted to light (5)
5. Long slice of wood (5)

ACROSS

1. Charles _ _ _ _ _ _ _ , author of
   A Christmas Carol (7)
5. Short for Susan (3)
6. Short for influenza (3)
7. These are often sprayed
   with deodorant (7)
10. J.K. _ _ _ _ _ _ _, author of the
    Harry Potter books (7)

DOWN

1. Hopelessness (7)
2. Thick, milky food loved by cats (5)
3. One of Santa's little helpers (3)
4. Dr. _ _ _ _ _, author of
   The Cat in the Hat (5)
8. Friend (3)
9. Most people have this many toes (3)

ACROSS

1. Medical professional (6)
5. Capital of Thailand (7)
7. Immediate (7)
10. Capital of Greece (6)

DOWN

1. Capital of Ireland (6)
2. Tin (3)
3. Tree that grows from an acorn (3)
4. Ice _ _ _ _ _ _, boots with blades underneath (6)
6. Belly (3)
8. Decided, fixed (3)
9. A gorilla, for example (3)

ACROSS

1. Fat sea animal with tusks (6)
5. Huge frozen chunk floating in the sea (7)
6. The little yellow servants of the supervillain in *Despicable Me* (7)
7. Someone who guides you to your seat at a play or a show (5)

DOWN

2. Area around the North Pole (6)
3. Bunnies (7)
4. Weird, peculiar (7)

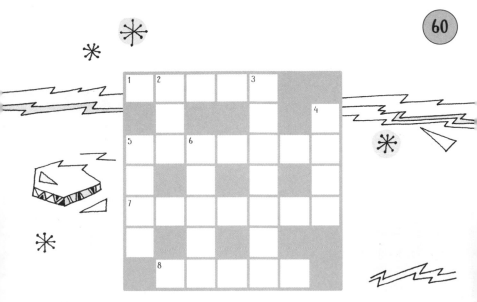

ACROSS

1. Drink noisily (5)
5. Common garden bird (7)
7. Santa enters your house down this (7)
8. Clips, cuts (5)

DOWN

2. Chop off (3)
3. Sweet, white root vegetable (7)
4. Move gently from side to side (4)
5. What Santa carries (4)
6. Creature from another planet (5)

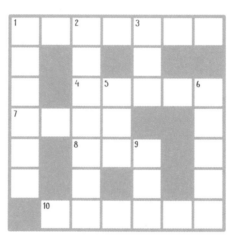

ACROSS

1. Uncovers (7)
4. Popular search engine (5)
7. Catch or tear your clothing on something (4)
8. Gain, receive (3)
10. Fiery mythical beast (6)

DOWN

1. Which country makes the Soyuz spacecraft which ferry astronauts to the International Space Station? (6)
2. This NASA space probe shares its name with the *Star Trek* ship captained by Kathryn Janeway (7)
3. Powdery remains left after something is burned (3)
5. Cavemen lived in the Stone ___ (3)
6. The star pattern also known as the Hunter (5)
9. Pull (3)

ACROSS

1. Shake with fear (7)
5. Push away, drive back (5)
6. Laugh out loud in text-speak (1.1.1.)
8. Unpiloted flying craft (5)
9. Motors (7)

DOWN

1. Insect that builds huge mounds (7)
2. Psychic power (1.1.1.)
3. A hot-air _____ (7)
4. Everlasting (7)
7. Opposite of off (2)
8. Four-legged friend (3)

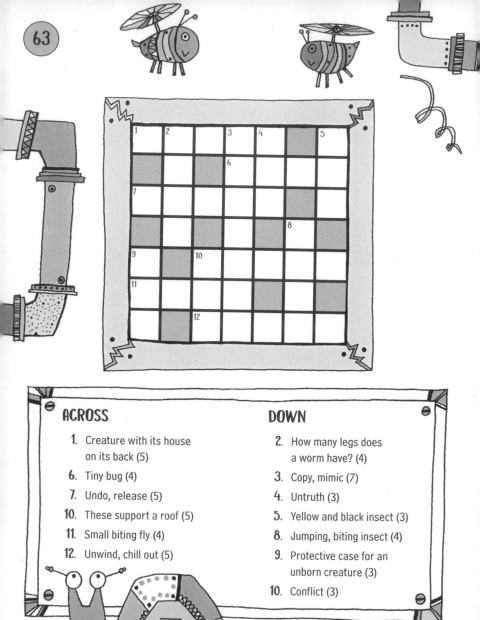

ACROSS

1. Creature with its house on its back (5)
6. Tiny bug (4)
7. Undo, release (5)
10. These support a roof (5)
11. Small biting fly (4)
12. Unwind, chill out (5)

DOWN

2. How many legs does a worm have? (4)
3. Copy, mimic (7)
4. Untruth (3)
5. Yellow and black insect (3)
8. Jumping, biting insect (4)
9. Protective case for an unborn creature (3)
10. Conflict (3)

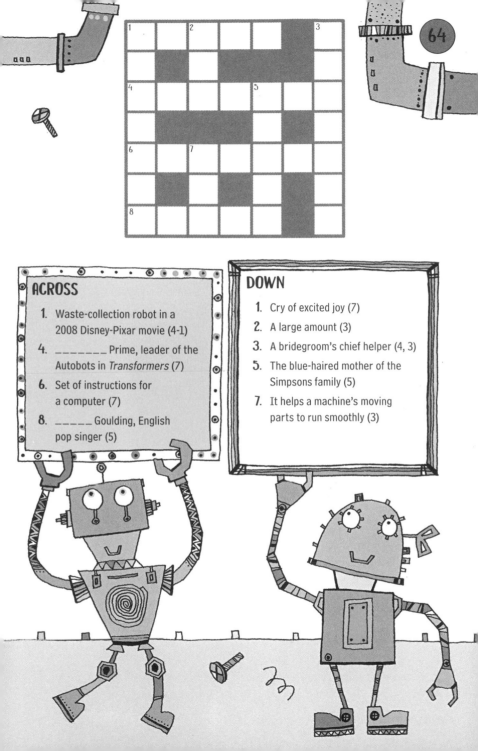

ACROSS

1. Waste-collection robot in a 2008 Disney-Pixar movie (4-1)
4. _ _ _ _ _ _ _ Prime, leader of the Autobots in *Transformers* (7)
6. Set of instructions for a computer (7)
8. _ _ _ _ _ Goulding, English pop singer (5)

DOWN

1. Cry of excited joy (7)
2. A large amount (3)
3. A bridegroom's chief helper (4, 3)
5. The blue-haired mother of the Simpsons family (5)
7. It helps a machine's moving parts to run smoothly (3)

65

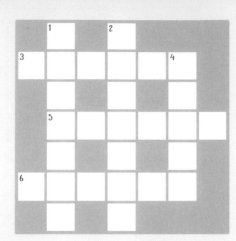

ACROSS

3. Tom _ _ _ _ _ _, best friend of Huckleberry Finn (6)
5. Rounded stone (6)
6. Shouted (6)

DOWN

1. Black and white crows (7)
2. Round thing in your head that lets you see (7)
4. Governed, controlled (5)

66

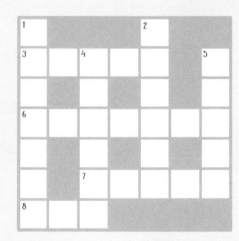

ACROSS

3. Leaf on Canada's flag (5)
6. Force that keeps you on the ground (7)
7. Someone banished as a punishment (5)
8. Devour (3)

DOWN

1. Dream up (7)
2. Star sign of the Twins (6)
4. Saturn, for example (6)
5. Herb that sounds like what a clock tells you (5)

ACROSS

2. Tall, long-beaked bird that hunts fish (5)
5. Opposite of departure (7)
6. Places to stay (6)

DOWN

1. Giant killed by David in the Bible (7)
3. Our home planet (5)
4. Sphere (4)

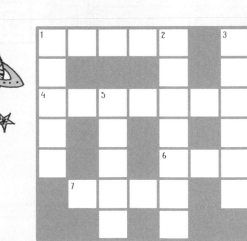

ACROSS

1. Star sign of the Ram (5)
4. Flying horse in Greek myth (7)
6. Adam's wife (3)
7. The star pattern known as the Plough or Big Dipper is part of the Great ＿＿＿＿ constellation (4)

DOWN

1. ＿＿＿＿＿ Centauri, the nearest star system to our own Solar System (5)
2. The Pleiades star cluster is also known as the Seven ＿＿＿＿＿＿＿ (7)
3. Star sign of the Fishes (6)
5. Star ＿＿＿＿＿, or astronomer (5)

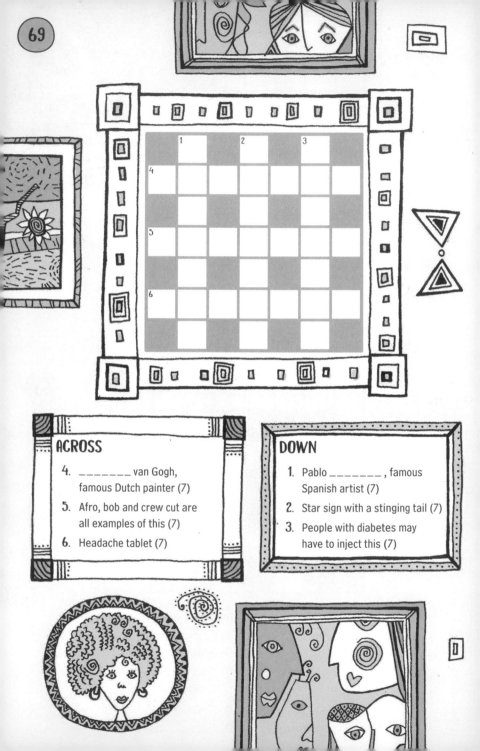

ACROSS

4. _ _ _ _ _ _ _ van Gogh, famous Dutch painter (7)
5. Afro, bob and crew cut are all examples of this (7)
6. Headache tablet (7)

DOWN

1. Pablo _ _ _ _ _ _ _ , famous Spanish artist (7)
2. Star sign with a stinging tail (7)
3. People with diabetes may have to inject this (7)

ACROSS

1. Chance, fortune (4)
5. _ _ _ _ _ _ _ Falls, famous waterfall on the US-Canadian border (7)
6. New _ _ _ _ _ _ _, largest city in Louisiana, USA, famed for its jazz music and lively Mardi Gras festival (7)
7. Children (4)

DOWN

1. Abraham _ _ _ _ _ _ _, famous US president (7)
2. Baby's crib (6)
3. Spectacles (7)
4. The 50th US state, a group of islands in the Pacific Ocean (6)

ACROSS

1. Where honey is made (7)
4. Stretchy material (7)
7. Mindless, undead people in horror movies (7)
8. Sorrow (7)

DOWN

1. Light winds (7)
2. Belonging to him (3)
3. Reasons given for not doing something (7)
5. Carrying weapons (5)
6. Two times (5)

72

ACROSS

1. Small, seedless orange (7)
4. Monkey-like animal from Madagascar (5)
6. Crunchy fruit (5)
7. Pig (3)
8. *The Jungle Book* is _ _ _ in India (3)

DOWN

1. Tummy (7)
2. Cup-shaped flower that comes in many shades (5)
3. Soft, juicy fruit (7)
5. Encounters (5)

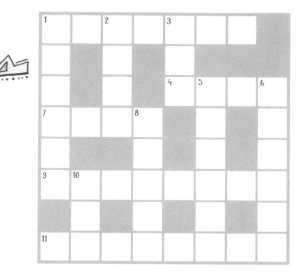

ACROSS

1. North American reindeer (7)
4. Sudden, shocked intake of breath (4)
7. It's worn by someone who is engaged (4)
9. Christmas chocolate rolls (4, 4)
11. _____ Lights, a glow in the sky also known as the Aurora Borealis (8)

DOWN

1. Jim _ _ _ _ _ _, Canadian comic actor, star of *The Grinch* (6)
2. Tumbledown building (4)
3. Insect (3)
5. Anybody (6)
6. Jail (6)
8. Welcome (5)
10. Flying saucer (1.1.1.)

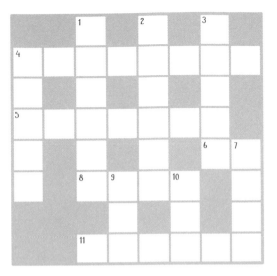

ACROSS

4. Canadian police on horses (8)
5. Bandits (7)
6. Hello (2)
8. Flatbread from India (4)
11. Canada's second main language, spoken especially in Quebec (6)

DOWN

1. First name of Canadian pop star Bieber, and Canadian prime minister Trudeau (6)
2. Capital of Canada (6)
3. Language of Wales (5)
4. Large Canadian deer (5)
7. What ants in your pants do (4)
9. Fire, water, earth and ___ (3)
10. Member of a women-only religious community (3)

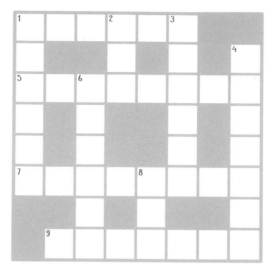

ACROSS

1. Vast North African desert (6)
5. Adventurer, pioneer (8)
7. Decoration (8)
9. Holy buildings (7)

DOWN

1. Two-speaker sound system (6)
2. Everything (3)
3. Reach a destination (6)
4. Gulps of air (7)
6. Son of a king or queen (6)
8. A 5 across could use one, or perhaps make one. (3)

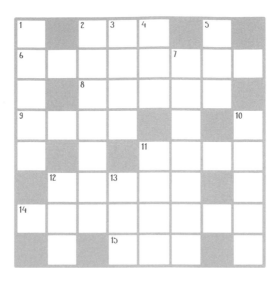

ACROSS

2. Number of players in a chess match (3)
6. Brave or admirable women (8)
8. Permit (5)
9. Small blast of air or smoke (4)
11. Grind up food with your teeth (4)
12. Walkway between chairs or supermarket shelves (5)
14. Gardens full of fruit trees (8)
15. Small hole in a needle (3)

DOWN

1. Outline (5)
2. Flow of vehicles (7)
3. Dog's wild ancestor (4)
4. Greasy liquid (3)
5. Long seat in a church (3)
7. The middle of _____, a very remote place (7)
10. Nationality of tennis star Roger Federer (5)
11. Stiff, sticky mud used to make pots and bricks (4)
12. Craft, skill (3)
13. "I asked Granny, and ___ said yes!" (3)

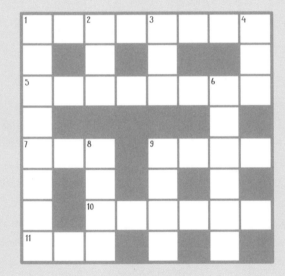

ACROSS

1. Blood-sucking monsters (8)
5. Ragged, falling apart (8)
7. The first part of many Scottish last names. It means "son of". (3)
9. You use these to kiss (4)
10. Small, six-legged creature (6)
11. Junior Boy Scout (3)

DOWN

1. Something in orange juice that helps to keep you healthy (7, 1)
2. Assembled, gathered (3)
3. Solid water (3)
4. Unhappy (3)
6. Anticipate (6)
8. Baby's bed (4)
9. The _ _ _ _ Boys, Peter Pan's young Neverland companions (4)

ACROSS

5. Month late in the year (8)
6. Varieties of tame animals (6)
8. Disaster, emergency (6)
9. The biggest land animal (8)

DOWN

1. Grabbed (8)
2. These flow when you cry (5)
3. Woodwind instruments (5)
4. Gifts (8)
6. Someone who cycles or rides a motorcycle a lot (5)
7. 2x2x2 (5)

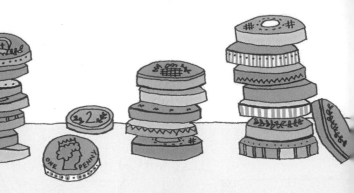

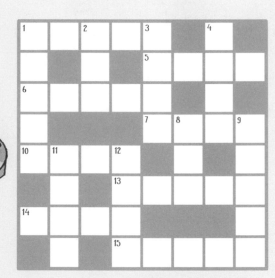

ACROSS

1. Regal (5)
5. Absent without leave (1.1.1.1.)
6. Small coin (5)
7. Evil deeds (4)
10. Amount of money owed (4)
13. Way, course (5)
14. Killer whale (4)
15. The UK's currency (5)

DOWN

1. Quick (5)
2. Japanese currency (3)
3. A hen ____ eggs (4)
4. Money that has been lent (4)
8. Note to show a 10 across (1.1.1.)
9. Use money (5)
11. Currency used by many European countries (4)
12. Catch, snare (4)

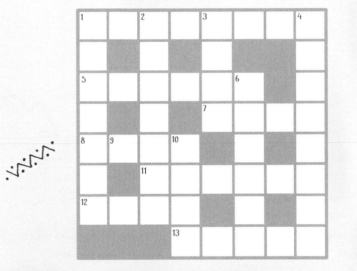

ACROSS

1. Public talks (8)
5. Furry, long-tailed water animals (6)
7. Small light (4)
8. Flower stalk (4)
11. Illusion seen in deserts (6)
12. Observes, notices (4)
13. Hot-tasting, like chili (5)

DOWN

1. Marriage partners (7)
2. Intense, to the limit (7)
3. Coil, ringlet (4)
4. Wet, hard to grasp (8)
6. Wildlife sightseeing trip in Africa (6)
10. Title for an unmarried woman (4)

ACROSS

1. Simple (4)
3. A plate of food (4)
6. Long story, poem or movie (4)
8. Used to choose your 3 across (4)
9. Nouns and verbs, for example (5)
12. Some bald people wear these (4)
14. ____ jackets, worn at sea (4)
16. Cats are said to have this many lives (4)
17. It covers your body (4)

DOWN

1. Not odd (4)
2. To slide over snow on long runners (3)
4. December 24 is Christmas ___ (3)
5. Noisy (4)
7. Christian symbol (5)
8. Award you wear around your neck (5)
10. One of two siblings born at the same time (4)
11. Enthusiastic (4)
13. ___-rummy, card game (3)
15. Liquid used for writing (3)

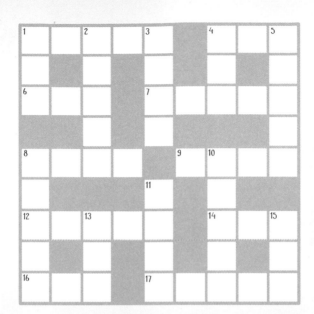

ACROSS

1. 25 x 2 (5)
4. Carpenter's tool (3)
6. Noise, racket (3)
7. Collection of songs or photos (5)
8. Fun knowledge test (4)
9. Rotate quickly (4)
12. Soil (5)
14. Girl's name (3)
16. At this time (3)
17. Calm, serenity (5)

DOWN

1. Trend, craze (3)
2. Mushrooms and toadstools (5)
3. Twelve months (4)
4. Weep out loud (3)
5. Adult female (5)
8. Female ruler (5)
10. Round Italian bread with toppings (5)
11. Large boat (4)
13. Uncooked (3)
15. Female sheep (3)

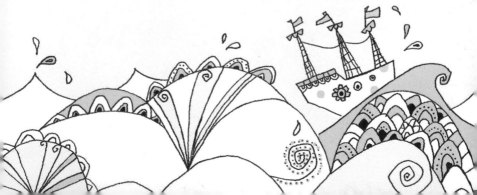

83

ACROSS

1. Once made by a spider, now found in a dusty corner (6)
5. Said at the end of a prayer (4)
6. Earth-moving vehicle (9)
8. She had a little lamb (4)
10. Short for street or saint (2)
12. Pearl-making shellfish (6)
14. Well-fed, satisfied (4)
15. Sir Lancelot, for example (6)

DOWN

1. Hair-grooming tool (4)
2. Healthy (4)
3. Large monkeys with long, dog-like muzzles (7)
4. Backwards (7)
7. Pale blue planet (6)
9. Yellow of an egg (4)
11. A horse's bouncing walk (4)
13. ___ boat, pulls ships into port (3)

ACROSS

1. Mischievous little goblins (4)
3. Hack (4)
7. Harry Potter's arch-enemy (9)
8. Magic words (6)
10. Make something illegal (3)
12. Requirements, essentials (5)
13. Blast, bang (9)

DOWN

1. What Harry Potter's magic cloak makes him (9)
2. Heartbeat (5)
4. Captain ____, Peter Pan's arch-enemy (4)
5. Magical mixtures created by a witch or wizard (7)
6. King Arthur's wizard (6)
9. Legendary apeman of the Himalayas (4)
11. Short sleep (3)

85

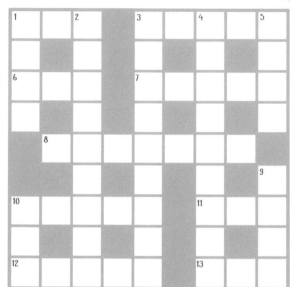

ACROSS

1. What you say when you jump out to scare someone (3)
3. Grip, clutch (5)
6. Pool or snooker stick (3)
7. Naming words (5)
8. Before (7)
10. German brothers who collected fairy tales (5)
11. A type of tree (3)
12. Fine cloth (5)
13. Outdoor game where you're "it" if you're caught (3)

DOWN

1. Johann Sebastian _ _ _ _, great German composer (4)
2. Surgery (9)
3. Ladies and _ _ _ _ _ _ _ _ (9)
4. You find rollercoasters at an _ _ _ _ _ _ _ _ park (9)
5. _ _ _ _-in-Boots, talking cat (4)
9. Self-satisfied (4)
10. You put this in your hair to style it (3)

ACROSS

1. Fuzzy, striped insect (9)
5. Many-legged creepy-crawlie (9)
6. The compass direction opposite to N.E. (1.1.)
8. Pincer-tailed brown insect (6)
10. British fighter pilots belong to this organization (1.1.1.)
11. Tool for gathering cut grass or fallen leaves (4)
14. Reusing waste (9)

DOWN

1. Slang for dollars (5)
2. Fluttering insect (9)
3. Ruler of an empire (7)
4. Finale (3)
7. Less good (5)
9. Irritate (3)
12. Muhammad ___, famous US boxer who died in 2016 (3)
13. At Easter, you might get a chocolate ___ (3)

87

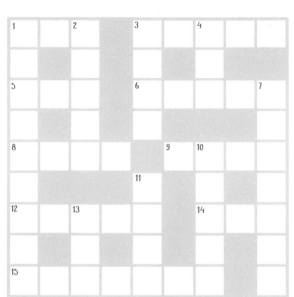

ACROSS

1. Angry crowd (3)
3. North African mountain range that shares its name with a book of maps (5)
5. Zero, nothing (3)
6. Part (5)
8. Cow meat (4)
9. Stare (4)
12. Foot joint (5)
14. Expected soon (3)
15. Gorges, ravines (7)

DOWN

1. Highest mountain in Western Europe; its name is "white mountain" in French (4, 5)
2. Swelling, bump (5)
3. Europe's longest mountain range (4)
4. Bruce ___, martial artist (3)
7. Highest mountain on Earth (7)
10. South America's longest mountain range (5)
11. Brave, admirable man (4)
13. Relatives (3)

ACROSS

1. Movie about the snowy adventures of some prehistoric animals (3, 3)
6. Grumpy green ogre who stars in a series of movies (5)
7. Give money (3)
8. Princess with magical powers in the movie *Frozen* (4)
10. Song of praise (4)
12. Faint, murky (3)
13. The cowboy hero of *Toy Story* (5)
15. National _ _ _ _ _ _, a country's theme song (6)

DOWN

2. Automobile (3)
3. Inquires (4)
4. Hollow (5)
5. Australian city, home to a famous opera house (6)
6. Firm, unmoving (6)
9. The young hero of *The Lion King* (5)
11. Kill a fly with a quick slap (4)
14. Rock mined for the minerals inside (3)

ACROSS

1. "The Big Bad Wolf huffed and he _ _ _ _ _ _." (6)

5. German boy's name that is spelled the same backwards (4)

6. Large, fast-flying water insect (9)

9. Growing your own flowers and vegetables (9)

13. Unwanted plant (4)

14. Gently come to rest (6)

DOWN

1. Pool, often with fish (4)

2. Kermit, for example (4)

3. "What goes up must come _ _ _ _." (4)

4. Taken, thieved (6)

7. Death's nickname is the Grim _ _ _ _ _ _ (6)

8. Thomas the Tank Engine's number (3)

10. Fathers (4)

11. Long-tailed water creature (4)

12. Sticky stuff (4)

ACROSS

1. Leafy plants smaller than trees (6)
5. Famous soccer player who played for 1 down (4)
6. United ____ Emirates, Middle-Eastern country (4)
8. In soccer, a kick awarded to a team fouled in a box around the goal (7)
11. More fortunate (7)
14. Authentic (4)
15. Shine, glimmer (5)
17. Field (6)

DOWN

1. South American national soccer team that has won many World Cups (6)
2. Hit with the palm of the hand (4)
3. Electronic sound-maker (7)
4. Plan, scheme (4)
7. David _____, world-famous soccer captain who married Posh Spice (7)
9. The card shown by a soccer referee as a first warning (6)
12. Hideous (4)
13. Tall, grass-like waterside plant (4)
16. What you call yourself (2)

NO SWIMMING

ACROSS

1. Leafy green herb used to make pesto (5)
4. Tap gently with your hand (3)
6. Very tall flower with a big, yellow head; you can eat its seeds (9)
7. Healthy eating plan (4)
8. Got bigger (4)
10. Wrong (9)
12. In French, *oui* – in Spanish, *si* (3)
13. Garbage, refuse (5)

DOWN

1. "The wheels on the ___ go round and round." (3)
2. Groups of words (9)
3. Big, sweet-smelling white flower (4)
4. Weak, unable to act (9)
5. Hurl, chuck (5)
7. Common flower with white petals and a yellow middle (5)
9. Front end of a ship (4)
11. What you do to your shoelaces (3)

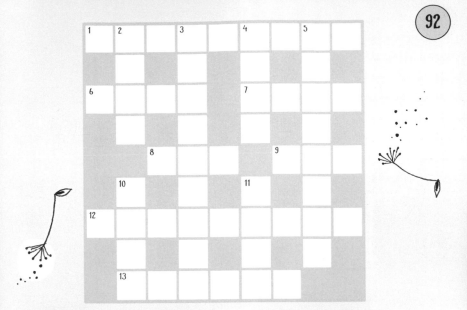

ACROSS

1. You leave food out for feathered garden visitors on this (4, 5)
6. Oven for baking clay pots (4)
7. Dark shade of blue (4)
8. Sweet ___, fragrant garden flower (3)
9. Insect that sounds like 4 down (3)
12. Paused, dithered (9)
13. Shrek's long-eared sidekick (6)

DOWN

2. Tall, elegant flower, or the ring around the pupil in the eye (4)
3. Common yellow-headed weed (9)
4. Parent's sister (4)
5. Scented plant with tiny purple flowers on spikes; used to make perfume (8)
10. A plant grows from this (4)
11. Herb, or wise person (4)

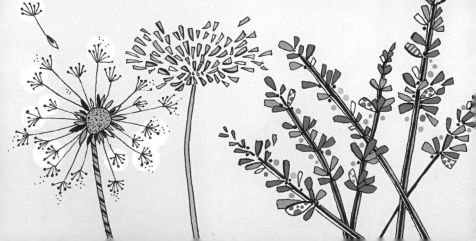

ACROSS

1. Magic stick (4)
3. Coat of _ _ _ _, on a knight's shield (4)
6. Main language of the Netherlands (5)
7. For what reason (3)
10. Buildings with turning sails (9)
12. Commander of a fleet of ships (7)
13. Traditional wooden shoe worn in the Netherlands (4)
14. Powerful divine beings (4)

DOWN

1. Woman whose husband has died (5)
2. Made up your mind (7)
4. To pull with oars (3)
5. Dark, salty Chinese sauce (3)
8. Netherlands region whose name is often used for the country itself (7)
9. "Every cloud has a silver _ _ _ _ _ _." (6)
11. Bugs Bunny's catchphrase: "What's up, _ _ _?" (3)
12. In the past (3)

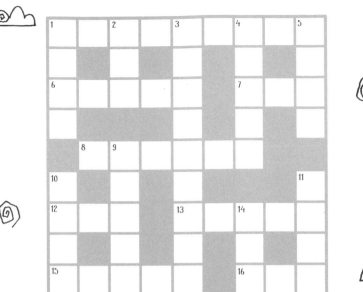

ACROSS

1. What did 10 down climb to reach the giant's castle? (9)
6. Sherlock Holmes lived at 221B _ _ _ _ _ Street (5)
7. Man, fellow (3)
8. 9 down befriended these little men (6)
12. _ _ _ Baba found the treasure cave of the Forty Thieves (3)
13. The number of 8 across that 9 down knew (5)
15. Work dough with your hands (5)
16. Little stand for a golfball (3)

DOWN

1. In which bear's bed was Goldilocks found sleeping? (4)
2. *Raiders of the Lost _ _ _*, Indiana Jones movie (3)
3. Startled (9)
4. Boy's name (5)
5. You use these to unlock things (4)
9. Snow _ _ _ _ _ was a beautiful princess who was hated by a vain, wicked queen (5)
10. In a fairy tale, which boy sold a cow for some magic beans? (4)
11. Most fairy tales begin with the words "_ _ _ _ upon a time..." (4)
14. Animal doctor (3)

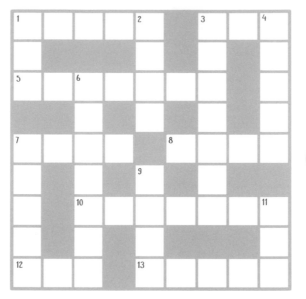

ACROSS

1. _ _ _ _ _ Baggins, the unlikely hero of *The Hobbit* (5)
3. A baby wears one at mealtimes (3)
5. Wizard who helps 1 across (7)
7. In *The Wonderful Wizard of Oz*, the name of Dorothy's dog (4)
8. In *The Lion, the Witch and the Wardrobe*, what kind of creature is Mr. Tumnus? (4)
10. These are used for drawing (7)
12. Sea fish (3)
13. _ _ _ _ _ Potter: his best friends are Ron and Hermione (5)

DOWN

1. In *The _ _ _*, by Roald Dahl, Sophie befriends a very large stranger (1.1.1.)
2. Friendly snowman in the movie *Frozen* (4)
3. American bison (7)
4. In *The Wonderful Wizard of Oz*, the Scarecrow is lacking a _ _ _ _ _. (5)
6. Observed (7)
7. Subject, theme (5)
9. Track, route (4)
11. Sneaky (3)

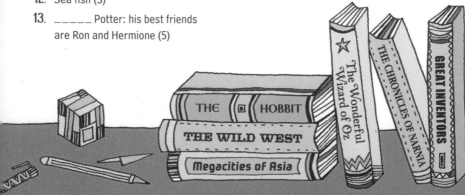

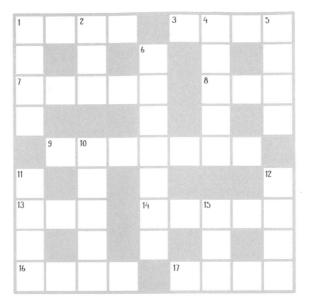

ACROSS

1. Alexander Graham ____, inventor of the telephone (4)
3. Round door handle (4)
7. Stinks, smells (5)
8. Small cake (3)
9. Louis _____, French inventor of a writing system for the blind (7)
13. Long-lived (3)
14. Light crown worn by a bride or princess (5)
16. Nose mucus (4)
17. Crooked (4)

DOWN

1. Last name of the Hungarian brothers who invented the ballpoint pen (4)
2. Tim Berners-___, English inventor of the World Wide Web (3)
4. Alfred _____ , Swedish inventor of dynamite. A famous prize shares his name. (5)
5. Karl ____, German inventor of the modern car, and co-founder of Mercedes-_____ (4)
6. Short-sleeved tops (1-6)
10. Player of music and talk broadcasts received over the airwaves (5)
11. Steve ____, founder of Apple Computers, or a word meaning careers (4)
12. James ____, Scottish inventor; the unit of electrical power shares his name. (4)
15. Fear and wonder (3)

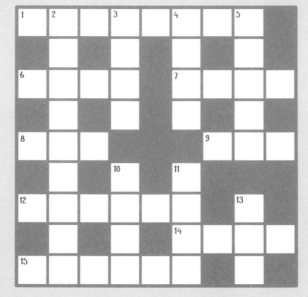

ACROSS

1. Table tennis (4, 4)
6. Recover from injury (4)
7. Wet weather (4)
8. The triple jump is also known as the ___, skip and jump. (3)
9. Number of events in a decathlon (3)
12. A downhill winter sport (6)
14. What you change on a bicycle when you go up or down a hill (4)
15. Rides a bike (6)

DOWN

2. Contact sport played on a rink (3, 6)
3. Sport played by Tiger Woods (4)
4. Used for rowing (4)
5. Slide smoothly along (5)
10. ____power, determination (4)
11. "Don't put all your ____ in one basket." (4)
13. Circuit in a race (3)

ACROSS

1. How many days did Jules Verne's Phileas Fogg take to travel around the world? (6)
5. You use it for baking (4)
6. Small carpet (3)
7. Strongly dislike (4)
9. Sounds like 1 down (3)
12. Number of horns on a unicorn (3)
14. On your own (4)
15. Tank, large container (3)
16. Number of holes in your head (4)
17. 1 across + 8 down (6)

DOWN

1. Number of corners on a cube (5)
2. Large rabbit relative (4)
3. Eastern form of exercise where you stretch and hold (4)
4. In this place (4)
8. The number of commandments that Moses gave (3)
10. When you halve a number, you divide it by ___ (3)
11. " _____ winks" is a short nap (5)
12. Leave out (4)
13. Divisible by two exactly (4)
14. Knock out (4)

ACROSS

1. In London, you can see a huge blue whale at the _ _ _ _ _ _ _ History Museum (7)
6. Globe, sphere (3)
7. Richard _ _ _ _ _ _ _, founder of the Virgin group of companies (7)
8. Happy (4)
9. Bend at the waist (3)
12. You can see paintings of famous people at London's National Portrait _ _ _ _ _ _ _ (7)
13. King and queen's daughter (8)

DOWN

2. This London square contains Nelson's Column, and shares its name with his greatest battle (9)
3. Baby biscuit (4)
4. Big ferris wheel on the South Bank of the River Thames (6, 3)
5. 1970s Swedish pop group (4)
7. London's famous clocktower (3, 3)
10. Scottish tribe (4)
11. Places to exercise (4)

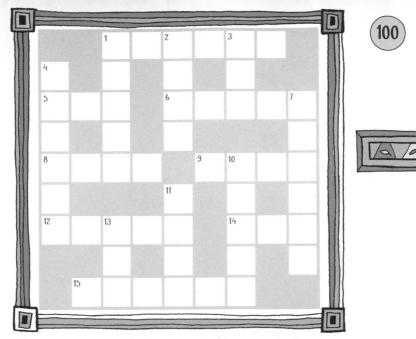

ACROSS

1. Tweetie Pie is this kind of songbird (6)
5. Female chicken (3)
6. Kitchen strainer (5)
8. Tiny brown bird with a loud call (4)
9. What birds lay (4)
12. Very large crow (5)
14. This bird is a symbol of wisdom (3)
15. Nose explosion (6)

DOWN

1. Small, narrow boat that you paddle (5)
2. US space agency (1.1.1.1.)
3. French for street (3)
4. Bathroom sprinkler (6)
7. Simply (6)
10. Large white farm bird (5)
11. Joint in your leg (4)
13. Dutch word meaning "from" found in names such as Vincent ___ Gogh (3)

ACROSS

1. Outdoor packed meal enjoyed by teddy bears (6)
5. Pile, mound (4)
6. Option (6)
8. Later (5)
10. Hospital caregiver (5)
14. Painter or sculptor (6)
15. *The Owl and the Pussycat*, for example (4)
16. Someone who checks and corrects books before they are printed (6)

DOWN

1. Group of wolves (4)
2. Someone who prepares food (4)
3. Head of a restaurant kitchen (4)
4. Someone who makes bread for a living (5)
7. Someone who explores underground (5)
9. Teacher (5)
11. Not different (4)
12. Scotsman's skirt (4)
13. Celebrity (4)

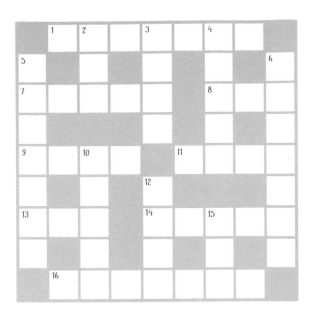

ACROSS

1. The largest ocean (7)
7. On top of, additional (5)
8. A female deer (3)
9. South American country where Paddington Bear was born (4)
11. Sunny, balmy (4)
13. Large country between Canada and Mexico (1.1.1.)
14. Country southwest of France (5)
16. Hug (7)

DOWN

2. In cartoon movies, both "Z" and "Flik" were one of these (3)
3. Middle Eastern country whose capital is Baghdad (4)
4. Large South Asian country where people ride elephants (5)
5. Kind, useful (7)
6. Where is Berlin the capital? (7)
10. Kingdom (5)
12. Russia used to be part of the Soviet Union. What initials stood for the Soviet Union's full name? (1.1.1.1.)
15. Curve (3)

ACROSS

1. In *Harry Potter*, the creatures that run Gringott's Bank (7)
5. The noise a cow makes (3)
6. Someone who turns into a hairy beast at the full moon (8)
10. Creepy, unsettling (6)
13. Is not (4)
14. Terror (4)
15. Unusual, foreign (6)

DOWN

1. A low, throaty sound, like an angry dog (5)
2. Sharp-tasting green fruit (4)
3. Happy emoticons :) (7)
4. Chunk of a tree (3)
7. May be written on gravestones (1.1.1.)
8. Dr. ___, owner of the TARDIS (3)
9. Room just below the roof (5)
10. Look for (4)
11. Shrek is one (4)
12. Short for kilogram (4)

ACROSS

1. Complete set of letters (8)
6. Idiot (4)
7. Top of a house (4)
9. Haul, drag (3)
10. Company symbol (4)
11. Short for Louis or Louise (3)
13. Steven _ _ _ _ _ _ _ _ _ ,
    US director of *E.T.* (9)
16. _ _ _ _ _ _ _ _ Cruz, Spanish
    actress and model (8)

DOWN

2. Star sign of the Lion (3)
3. October festival of
   tricks and treats (9)
4. Half-robot race in *Star Trek* (4)
5. As well (3)
6. Creases (5)
8. Threw (5)
12. In the Bible, Cain's brother (4)
14. Burst (3)
15. Eminem's music style (3)

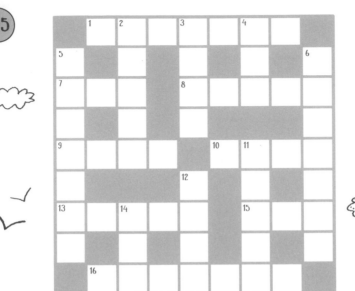

ACROSS

1. African animal with a very long neck (7)
7. Function, purpose (3)
8. East African country famous for its big game reserves (5)
9. Sharks are big _ _ _ _ (4)
10. Opposite of false (4)
13. Cowboy's looped rope (5)
15. I will (3)
16. African wild pig with a long, bumpy snout and curling tusks (7)

DOWN

2. Things, objects (5)
3. Requests (4)
4. Entertaining (3)
5. African wild cow with large, curling horns (7)
6. Swift African antelope (7)
11. Thick-skinned African animal with horns on its nose (5)
12. Usain _ _ _ _, record-breaking Jamaican sprinter (4)
14. Health resort (3)

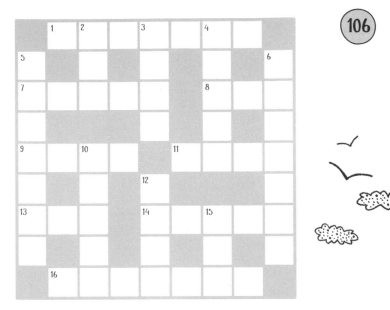

ACROSS

1. African mongoose that stands upright to keep watch over its burrow (7)
7. Scavenging, dog-like African animal with a laugh-like call (5)
8. Charge, payment (3)
9. Omelettes are made from these (4)
11. Move wings up and down (4)
13. Fitting, appropriate (3)
14. Go inside (5)
16. Flightless, running African bird, the biggest of all birds (7)

DOWN

2. Used for seeing (3)
3. The noise a lion makes (4)
4. Terrible (5)
5. African big cat, the fastest land animal (7)
6. African big cat with spots (7)
10. Bill _ _ _ _ _, billionnaire founder of Microsoft (5)
12. One who inherits (4)
15. Uncontrollable face twitch (3)

ACROSS

1. Fastened (6)
5. The noise a pig makes (4)
6. Science that may use test tubes and Bunsen burners (9)
8. As well (4)
10. Beams, shafts (4)
12. Coal, for example (4)
13. Costume (6)

DOWN

1. Common metal beginning with "z" (4)
2. High school dance (4)
3. Little circles (4)
4. Power (6)
7. Gas used to fill party balloons (6)
9. Capital of Norway (4)
10. Smallest animal of a litter (4)
11. Tiny white crystals added to food (4)

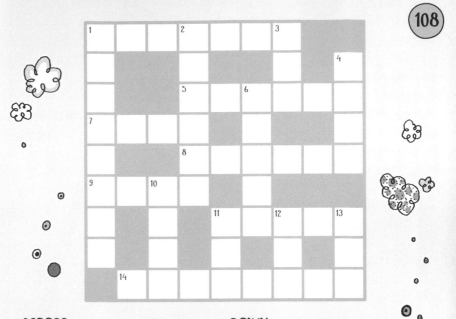

ACROSS

1. Chemical element found in milk that strengthens your teeth and bones (7)
5. Shelled sea reptile (6)
7. Expel, kick out (4)
8. Chemical element we breathe (6)
9. Common metal (4)
11. Leafy forest plants (5)
14. The most common element; it is found in water (8)

DOWN

1. Chemical element used to disinfect swimming pools (8)
2. Cloth, thread (6)
3. You wipe your shoes on this (3)
4. Gas element used to fill luminous tubes in advertising signs (4)
6. Rolls _ _ _ _ _, luxury car (5)
10. Alright (4)
11. China and Japan are in the _ _ _ East (3)
12. Old piece of cloth (3)
13. _ _ _ Francisco, American city (3)

ACROSS

1. Pig-like rainforest animal (5)
5. Frequently (5)
6. Crazy (3)
8. Small branches that sprout leaves (5)
9. Huge, green South American snake (8)
13. Damp (5)
14. Very slow South American animal that spends most of its life hanging upside-down in trees (5)

DOWN

1. Club, side (4)
2. Poke (4)
3. A tree uses this to get water from the ground (4)
4. Pleaded (6)
7. Huge South American rainforest and river (6)
10. Scratches, scrapes (4)
11. Roman emperor (4)
12. Curved support structure (4)

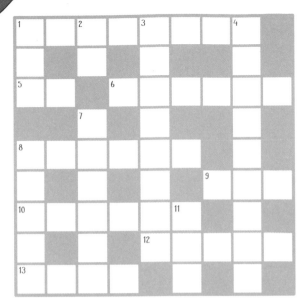

ACROSS

1. (with 1 down) Snake-like South American fish that gives quite a shock (8, 3)
5. Short for Los Angeles (1.1.)
6. Toxic substance (6)
8. Extremely sad, terrible (6)
9. Short for advertisements (3)
10. Rainforest bird with a huge, bright beak (6)
12. Deep serving spoon (5)
13. Ride the waves on a board (4)

DOWN

1. (see 1 across)
2. For example (1.1.)
3. _____ fish are kept in warm-water tanks (8)
4. Huge, snapping reptile (9)
7. Powerful, spotted South American big cat (6)
8. Ballerinas' skirts (5)
11. Pester (3)

ACROSS

1. Seasonal storm in India (7)
6. New _ _ _ _ _, India's capital (5)
7. Darjeeling and Assam are types of this from India (3)
8. Name given to the Indian movie industry (9)
11. 1+2+3+4 (3)
12. _ _ _ Solo, pilot in *Star Wars* (3)
13. Most of the world's supply of these sweet, juicy fruits comes from India (7)

DOWN

2. Grease (3)
3. Reflective (5)
4. Grain used to make a hot, mushy breakfast dish (3)
5. Mahatma _ _ _ _ _ _, famous Indian leader (6)
6. Discussion (6)
9. Sri _ _ _ _ _, island-nation south of India (5)
10. Measurement of weight: there are 16 in a pound (5)
12. Cuddle (3)

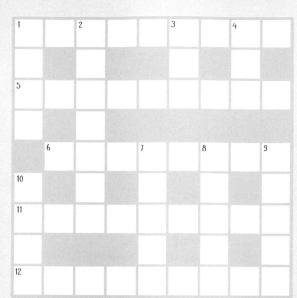

ACROSS

1. Small tornado (9)
5. Blizzard (9)
6. Lose (8)
11. Often goes with thunder (9)
12. Very good (9)

DOWN

1. Stinging yellow and black insect (4)
2. Pressing clothes to remove creases (7)
3. Damp, moist (3)
4. "I drink neither tea ___ coffee." (3)
7. Part of a flower (5)
8. Athletic, nimble (5)
9. Number of legs on an octopus (5)
10. Run away (4)

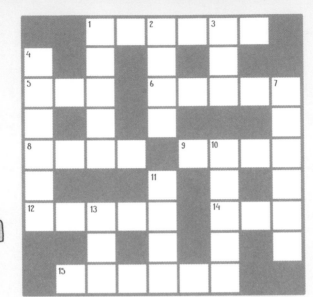

ACROSS

1. Europe's second-longest river (6)
5. Goal, target (3)
6. Guesthouse (5)
8. Gently shine (4)
9. Squat, warty, frog-like creature (4)
12. River flowing through Paris (5)
14. You hear with this (3)
15. Longest river in the UK (6)

DOWN

1. Disney's flying elephant (5)
2. Egypt's great river (4)
3. The bottom of a river (3)
4. Sacred river of India (6)
7. Persist, carry on (6)
10. Vast expanse of salt water (5)
11. In a Disney movie, orphan boy who befriends a dragon named Elliot (4)
13. ___ cream (3)

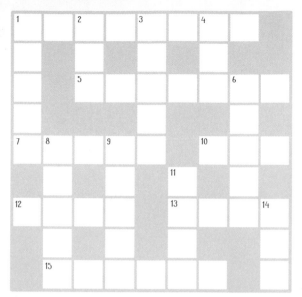

ACROSS

1. Famous portrait by Leonardo da Vinci in the Louvre Museum, Paris (4, 4)
5. The _ _ _ _ _ _ _ of the Opera, novel and musical set in Paris (7)
7. French pancake (5)
10. Very popular song (3)
12. Martial art (4)
13. Elsa's sister in the Disney movie *Frozen* (4)
15. The _ _ _ _ _ _ Tower, Paris's top landmark (6)

DOWN

1. Supernatural power (5)
2. Pinch, bite (3)
3. Go away (5)
4. "The cat _ _ _ on the mat." (3)
6. Vegetable that makes you cry (5)
8. Blusher; French for "red" (5)
9. Confirmation (5)
11. Place to eat and drink (4)
14. _ _ _ de Triomphe, a famous arch in Paris (3)

TROCADÉRO

MÉTRO PASSY

ÎLE AU CYGNES

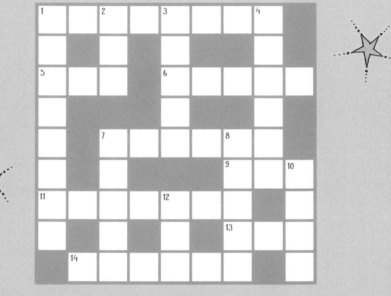

ACROSS

1. Where would you go in New York City to catch a show? (8)
5. Obtain (3)
6. Unlocks (5)
7. The _ _ _ _ _ State Building was climbed by King Kong in the movies (6)
9. What you say to attract attention (3)
11. The Statue of _ _ _ _ _ _ _ stands on an island in New York Bay (7)
13. Cut grass (3)
14. The Brooklyn _ _ _ _ _ _ connects Brooklyn to Manhattan Island (6)

DOWN

1. New York City's fruity nickname (3, 5)
2. Choose (3)
3. Sag, wilt (5)
4. New York's baseball team play at the _ _ _ _ _ _ Stadium (6)
7. Cinder, glowing coal (5)
8. What "ants" and "pants" do (5)
10. You do this when you're tired or bored (4)
12. Pole, staff (3)

ACROSS

1. Used for drawing (6)
5. Sound that bounces back (4)
6. Region, district (4)
7. Governors (6)
9. Admission slip (6)
11. Bee house (4)
12. In the near future (4)
13. What you use with a needle (6)

DOWN

1. 2 down works as a journalist for the *Daily* _ _ _ _ _ _ (6)
2. Superman's secret identity (5, 4)
3. Superman's arch-enemy (3, 6)
4. Norse god of thunder who joins the Avengers superhero team (4)
8. What Captain America uses to protect himself and knock out enemies (6)
10. Tony Stark is the real name of _ _ _ _ Man (4)

ACROSS

1. Snakes (8)
7. Decay (3)
8. C.S. _____, author of *The Lion, the Witch and the Wardrobe* (5)
9. What makes sailing ships go (4)
12. The first European to reach Australia was Captain James ____ (4)
14. _____ 11, the space mission that took the first people to the Moon, was named after the Greek god of the Sun. (6)
16. Long journey, hike (4)
17. The opposite of B.C. (1.1.)

DOWN

2. Consumed (5)
3. Marco _____, explorer from Venice who wrote about his travels in Asia (4)
4. Name given to the American continents by 16th Century European explorers (3, 5)
5. Distress signal (1.1.1.)
6. Team of sailors (4)
10. What elephants' tusks are made from (5)
11. Sir Francis _____, vice-admiral of the fleet that defeated the Spanish Armada (5)
13. Ways of tying ropes (5)
15. Dull, clumsy person (3)

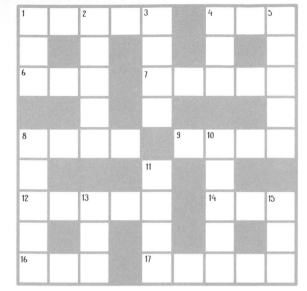

ACROSS

1. Tree with red berries and prickly leaves used in Christmas decorations (5)
4. Tree that sounds like something burned (3)
6. ___ tree, also known as eucalyptus (3)
7. Large, spreading, conifer tree with fragrant wood (5)
8. & 9. Scaly seed-capsule that grows on many evergreen trees (4, 4)
12. Towering, soaring (5)
14. What you say when you make a wedding vow (1, 2)
16. Polite way to address a man you don't know (3)
17. Greek island (5)

DOWN

1. Witch (3)
2. Sour yellow fruit (5)
3. Cry of disgust (4)
4. First ___, emergency help (3)
5. Animal you ride (5)
8. The flat parts of your hands (5)
10. Mediterranean tree whose small, fleshy fruit is often pickled, or pressed for its oil (5)
11. Short for synchronize (4)
13. Tall conifer tree (3)
15. Be in debt (3)

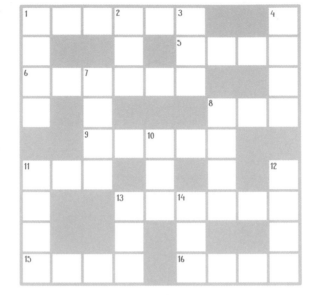

ACROSS

1. Soft, holey washing aid (6)
5. Unit of area about the size of a soccer field (4)
6. Shellfish that clings tightly to rocks (6)
8. In Wonderland, Alice meets the grinning Cheshire _ _ _ (3)
9. Slow, shelled, legless creature (5)
11. Slice, chop (3)
13. Someone who chooses to live alone, far from other people (6)
15. Worm on a hook (4)
16. Greasy (4)

DOWN

1. Given away for money (4)
2. Short sleep (3)
3. Dine (3)
4. Writing (4)
7. Sail-pole (4)
8. Shellfish whose two-part shell shuts very tightly (4)
10. Playing card (3)
11. Sea creature that walks sideways (4)
12. Stop over, visit (4)
13. Shed (3)
14. _ _ _ de Janeiro, capital of Brazil (3)

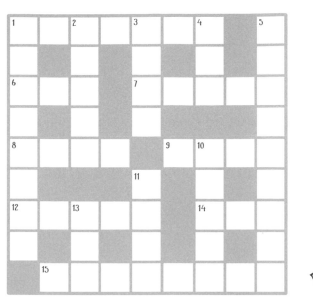

ACROSS

1. Underwater plant (7)
6. As well as (3)
7. Long throwing weapon (5)
8. Rage (4)
9. Hot, liquid rock (4)
12. Japanese rice rolls often served stuffed with raw fish (5)
14. Sick (3)
15. Sea _ _ _ _ _ _ _ _ , flower-like creatures found in tide pools (8)

DOWN

1. Five-armed sea creature (8)
2. A snake that sounds like it should be good at mathematics (5)
3. The direction the Earth turns (4)
4. Cease to live (3)
5. Tiny shellfish that grow in a crust on the undersides of ships (9)
10. Line up (5)
11. Stable, solid (4)
13. Male child (3)

ACROSS

1. Curly-haired dog (6)
5. Boatyard (4)
6. Dog bred to fetch things, such as a Labrador or Golden _ _ _ _ _ _ _ _ _ (9)
8. Thin racing dog (9)
12. Gemstone (4)
13. Heroic dog in books and movies (6)

DOWN

1. Raised walkway above the sea (4)
2. Word that starts a letter (4)
3. Boundary (4)
4. TV, monitor (6)
7. A continent (6)
9. Shout, holler (4)
10. If you're unlikely to achieve something, the _ _ _ _ are against you. (4)
11. Great _ _ _ _ , tall dog breed (4)

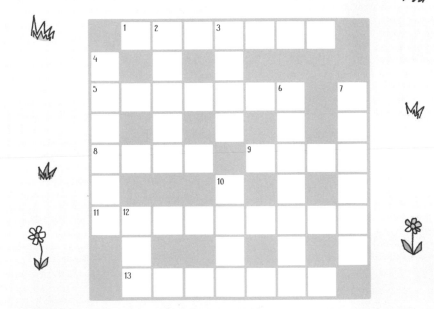

ACROSS

1. King _ _ _ _ _ _ _ Spaniel (7)
5. Jack _ _ _ _ _ _ _, small breed of terrier (7)
8. Short for mayonnaise (4)
9. _ _ _ _ *Trek*, featuring Captain Kirk and Mr. Spock (4)
11. Huge, hairy spider (9)
13. Young dogs (7)

DOWN

2. Arctic sled dog (5)
3. The part of a fishing rod where you wind the line (4)
4. Inventor Wallace's faithful dog (6)
6. Green salad vegetable (7)
7. _ _ _ _ _ _ Shepherd, or Alsatian (6)
10. Crack, break (4)
12. Short for amplifier (3)

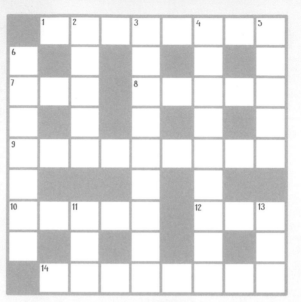

ACROSS

1. Indian birds with big, fanned tails (8)
7. Also known as (1.1.1.)
8. Christmas song (5)
9. Huge, white Arctic carnivore (5, 4)
10. Star sign of the Scales (5)
12. Lid, cap (3)
14. Water creature with an upright body and curly tail (8)

DOWN

2. Electronic mail (5)
3. Big, tough, brown insect pest found especially in warmer countries (9)
4. Someone who works with wood (9)
5. _ _ _ _ _ power, energy from the Sun (5)
6. Baby frog or toad (7)
11. Spelling _ _ _, word-power contest (3)
13. Baked dish covered in pastry (3)

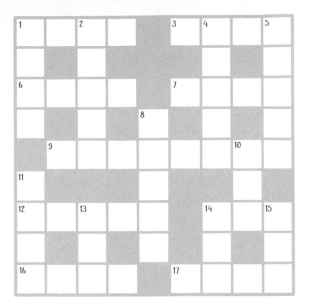

ACROSS

1. Nothing, zilch (4)
3. Sector, area (4)
6. Idle, sluggish (4)
7. Dopey, dreamy (4)
9. Most insane (8)
12. Surprise, dazzle (5)
14. Zig___, jagged line (3)
16. Spots, acne (4)
17. Shoot off like a rocket (4)

DOWN

1. South African tribe (4)
2. Shaving blade (5)
4. The _ _ _ _ _ layer protects the Earth from harmful rays (5)
5. Country where Tutankhamun's tomb was discovered (5)
8. Medieval Mexican civilization who built pyramid temples (5)
10. The Baltic or Caspian, for example (3)
11. A type of music where the players make it up as they go along (4)
13. Perform in a play or movie (3)
14. Wildlife park (3)
15. You chew this, but don't eat it (3)

1

```
F O A L
A   L   S
C H I C K
T   V   I
S L E E P
```

2

```
  L A M B
C R   U
A N G R Y
L   U   S
F R E T
```

3

```
S U P E R
E   R
T A I L S
    C U
D R E A M
```

4

```
  C R A M
T O E   A
    R E A R
R A F T S
  L   E
```

5

```
F I S H
O   C A P
A L A S
M A N T A
  W   Y
```

6

```
C A T   F
O   H   U
C L O W N
O   R   N
A N N O Y
```

7

```
D I S C O
  T   D
A H E A D
D   E
D E P T H
```

8

```
C O N G A
A   A   G
R A I S E
E   L   S
D I S C
```

9

```
T W I S T
U   D   A
S W E E P
K   A
S A L S A
```

10

```
C U B E
H   L   B
A W A R E
R   Z   A
T W E E T
```

11

```
A   T   S
C L O A K
T   U   U
O R G A N
R   H   K
```

12

```
S C A L E
  E   A
F L U T E
  L   E
D O O R S
```

13

```
C A L L
A   E A R
L O S T
M U S I C
  T   N
```

14

```
P I A N O
O   M   A
P I P E S
    L   I
W E E K S
```

15

```
G A S   I
O   P I T
L   A   A
F A R   L
  K E Y
```

16

```
W H E E L
A   L   U
T U D O R
C   E   K
H O R N
```

17

```
M I N T
I   O   A
M O T O R
E   E   M
S A D L Y
```

18

```
G R I E F
P   C   O
S T E E R
  W   K
F O C U S
```

19

```
  M O A N
S O U R
N O T E S
O N E   U
W   R U N
```

20

```
R A C E
I   O   S
C O M E T
H   I   A
  S C A R
```

21

```
L U N A R
O   A   I
V E N U S
E   N   E
  B Y E
```

22

```
  K
S W I F T
W   T   H
A R E N A
N   S   W
```

23

```
  I C O N
L   R   O
A W A K E
R   N   L
K N E W
```

24

```
M A C A W
O   O   I
R O B I N
S       C
E A G L E
```

25

```
  I S P Y
X   I   O
M U M M Y
A   O   O
S I N K
```

26

```
S   N   I
C H E S S
O   I   L
R O G U E
E   H   S
```

27

```
P O K E R
A   I   E
W O N K A
N   G   D
S       Y
```

28

```
S I L K
T   E   A
E I G H T
M   A   O
  P L U M
```

29

A	N	G	E	L
	U		A	
A	W	A	R	D
I		R		
R	I	D	E	R

30

F	I	B		F
E		O		L
W	H	A	L	E
E		T		E
R		S	I	T

31

C	A	W		B
A	S	I	D	E
M	I	N	E	R
E	A	G	E	R
L		S	P	Y

32

M	O	C	H	A
A		O		M
K	E	B	A	B
E		R		L
S	H	A	D	E

33

C			N	
R	I	C	E	
O		O	W	L
F		W		A
T	A	S	T	Y

34

K	O	R	E	A
I		E		J
C	H	I	N	A
K		G		R
S	A	N	K	

35

	G			S	
C	A	R	R	O	T
	R		I		O
C	L	O	V	E	R
	I		E		M
S	C	A	R	E	S

36

R	A	D	I	S	H
I		A			A
B		T	U	R	N
B	E	A	N		D
O			I		L
N	E	T	T	L	E

37

P	A	C	I	N	G
E		U		U	
P	O	T	A	T	O
P		E		M	
E	A	R	N	E	D
R				G	

38

C		G		M	
A	M	U	S	E	D
C		A		D	
T	U	R	N	I	P
U		D		U	
S	E	S	A	M	E

39

Q	U	I	V	E	R
U		N		L	
A	R	C	H	E	R
R		O		V	
R	A	M	M	E	D
Y		E		N	

40

H	U	N	G	E	R
O		E			A
O		S	T	E	P
V	O	T	E		I
E			L	I	D
S	O	I	L		S

41

R	O	B	I	N	
O		A		U	
W	A	R	M	T	H
	H		E		O
T	O	M	A	T	O
	Y		N		D

42

W	E	T		I	V	Y
O		A		N		U
K	I	N	G	D	O	M
	G		I			
V	O	L	C	A	N	O
O		E		N		A
W	A	D		A	I	R

43

O	C	T	O	B	E	R
U		U		A		
G	E	E		T	O	M
H		S		T		E
T	O	D	D	L	E	R
	A		E		R	
M	A	Y		S	K	Y

44

	K	O	A	L	A	
W		U		A		A
A	N	T		R	I	M
V		B	A	G		B
E	R	A		E	M	U
S		C		S		S
	S	K	E	T	C	H

45

R	I	P	P	E	D	
O		A		X		
B	I	C	Y	C	L	E
O		K		I		R
T	R	A	C	T	O	R
		G		E		O
	L	E	A	D	E	R

46

P	I	R	A	T	E	S
O		Y			O	
R		F	E	D		A
T	A	R		Y	A	P
	R	O	G	E	R	
	T		O		M	
		T	O	W		

47

C	A	N	A	D	A	
L		E			G	
I	M	P	L	I	E	D
M		A		R		U
B	E	L	G	I	U	M
	N			S		P
	D	I	S	H	E	S

48

W		M		C		P
I	R	O	N	A	G	E
N		U		M		A
D	U	N	G	E	O	N
S		D		L		U
O			M	O	A	T
R	A	M		T		S

49

P	Y	R	A	M	I	D
O		O		E		
E	Q	U	A	T	O	R
T		T		H		O
S	A	I	L	O	R	S
	N		D		E	
G	U	E	S	S	E	S

50

	S	Y	M	B	O	L
B		A			W	
A	C	C	O	U	N	T
R		H		B		E
N	A	T	I	O	N	S
	R		A		T	
S	K	I	R	T	S	

51

C	L	I	M	A	T	E
U		C			W	
R	A	I	N	B	O	W
R		C		R		A
E	C	L	A	I	R	S
N		E		D		H
T	O	S	S	E	D	

52

G	R	A	P	E	S	
	A		E		M	
T	I	T	A	N	I	C
	S		C		L	
M	I	C	H	A	E	L
	N		H		I	
	S	Q	U	A	R	E

53
```
O R I G A M I
  E   L   E
S A M U R A I
  D   M   S
R E D   S U N
  R       R
  S H A R E
```

54
```
A S H O R E
C   A   E   G
C E N T A U R
E   S   L   E
P R E D I C T
T   L   Z   E
      W E L L
```

55
```
R I C H A R D
E   A   R   E
P E T E R   L
E   C   A   A
A   H E N R Y
T   E   G   E
S U S P E N D
```

56
```
H O P E S   M
    H   H   O
P E A S A N T
L   R   D   H
A M A Z O N S
N   O   W
K   H O S T S
```

57
```
D I C K E N S
E   R   L   E
S U E   F L U
P   A   A   S
A R M P I T S
I   A   E
R O W L I N G
```

58
```
D O C T O R
U   A   A   S
B A N G K O K
L   U   U   A
I N S T A N T
N   E   P   E
  A T H E N S
```

59
```
W A L R U S
    R   A   T
I C E B E R G
    T   B   A
M I N I O N S
    C   T   G
      U S H E R
```

60
```
S L U R P
    O   A   S
S P A R R O W
A   L   S   A
C H I M N E Y
K   E   I
  S N I P S
```

61
```
R E V E A L S
U   O   S
S   Y A H O O
S N A G   R
I   G E T   I
A   E   U   O
  D R A G O N
```

62
```
T R E M B L E
E   S   A   N
R E P E L   D
M   L   L O L
I   D R O N E
T   O   O   S
E N G I N E S
```

63
```
S N A I L   B
  O   M I T E
U N T I E   E
  E   T   F
E   W A L L S
G N A T   E
G   R E L A X
```

64
```
W A L L E   B
H   O       E
O P T I M U S
O       A   T
P R O G R A M
E   I   G   A
E L L I E   N
```

65
```
  M   E
S A W Y E R
  G   E   U
  P E B B L E
  I   A   E
Y E L L E D
  S   L
```

66
```
I     G
M A P L E   T
A   L   M   H
G R A V I T Y
I   N   N   M
N   E X I L E
E A T
```

67
```
      G
H E R O N
  A   L   B
A R R I V A L
  T   A   L
  H O T E L S
      H
```

68
```
A R I E S   P
L       I   I
P E G A S U S
H   A   T   C
A   Z   E V E
  B E A R S
      R   S
```

69
```
  P   S   I
V I N C E N T
  C   O   S
H A I R C U T
  S   P   L
A S P I R I N
  O   O   N
```

70
```
L U C K   G
I   R   H   L
N I A G A R A
C   D   W   S
O R L E A N S
L   E   I   E
N   K I D S
```

71
```
B E E H I V E
R   I   I   X
E L A S T I C
E   R   W   U
Z O M B I E S
E   E   C   E
S A D N E S S
```

72

```
S A T S U M A
T   U       P
O   L E M U R
M   I   E   I
A P P L E   C
C       T   O
H O G   S E T
```

73

C	A	R	I	B	O	U
A	U		U			
R		I		G	A	S	P
R	I	N	G		N		R
E			R		Y		I
Y	U	L	E	L	O	G	S
	F		E		N		O
N	O	R	T	H	E	R	N

74

		J		O		W
M	O	U	N	T	I	E	S
O		S		T		L
O	U	T	L	A	W	S
S		I		W		H	I
E		N	A	A	N		T
		I		U		C
	F	R	E	N	C	H

75

S	A	H	A	R	A
T		L		R		B
E	X	P	L	O	R	E	R
R		R		I		E
E		I		V		A
O	R	N	A	M	E	N	T
		C		A		H
	T	E	M	P	L	E	S

76

S		T	W	O		P
H	E	R	O	I	N	E	S
A		A	L	L	O	W
P	U	F	F		W		S
E		F		C	H	E	W
	A	I	S	L	E		I
O	R	C	H	A	R	D	S
	T		E	Y	E	S

77

V	A	M	P	I	R	E	S
I		E		C		A
T	A	T	T	E	R	E	D
A				X
M	A	C		L	I	P	S
I		R		O		E
N		I	N	S	E	C	T
C	U	B		T		T

78

S		T		O		P
N	O	V	E	M	B	E	R
A		A		O		E
T		B	R	E	E	D	S
C	R	I	S	I	S		E
H		K		G		N
E	L	E	P	H	A	N	T
D		R		T		S

79

R	O	Y	A	L		L
A		E		A	W	O	L
P	E	N	N	Y		A
I			S	I	N	S
D	E	B	T		O		P
	U		R	O	U	T	E
O	R	C	A			N
	O		P	O	U	N	D

80

S	P	E	E	C	H	E	S
P		X		U		L
O	T	T	E	R	S		I
U		R		L	A	M	P
S	T	E	M		F		P
E		M	I	R	A	G	E
S	E	E	S		R		R
		S	P	I	C	Y

81

E	A	S	Y		M	E	A	L
V	K				V		O
E	P	I	C		M	E	N	U
N			R		E		D
		W	O	R	D	S
T		S		A		K
W	I	G	S		L	I	F	E
I		I			N		E
N	I	N	E		S	K	I	N

82

F	I	F	T	Y		S	A	W
A		U		E		O		O
D	I	N		A	L	B	U	M
		G		R				A
Q	U	I	Z		S	P	I	N
U			S		I
E	A	R	T	H		Z	O	E
E		A		I		Z		W
N	O	W		P	E	A	C	E

83

C	O	B	W	E	B		R
O		E		A	M	E	N
M		L		B		V
B	U	L	L	D	O	Z	E	R
	R			O		R
M	A	R	Y		N		S	T
	N		O	Y	S	T	E	R
F	U	L	L			U		O
	S		K	N	I	G	H	T

84

I	M	P	S		C	H	O	P
N		U		M		O		O
V	O	L	D	E	M	O	R	T
I		S		R		K		I
S	P	E	L	L	S			O
I			I		Y		N
B	A	N		N	E	E	D	S
L		A				T
E	X	P	L	O	S	I	O	N

85

B	O	O		G	R	A	S	P
A		P	E		M		U
C	U	E		N	O	U	N	S
H		R		T		S		S
	E	A	R	L	I	E	R
	T		E		M		S
G	R	I	M	M		E	L	M
E		O		E		N		U
L	I	N	E	N		T	A	G

86

B	U	M	B	L	E	B	E	E
U		U		M		N
C	E	N	T	I	P	E	D	E
K		T		E
S	W		E	A	R	W	I	G
O		R		O		R
R	A	F		R	A	K	E
S		L			L		G
R	E	C	Y	C	L	I	N	G

87

M	O	B		A	T	L	A	S
O		U		L		F
N	I	L		P	I	E	C	E
T		G		S				V
B	E	E	F		G	A	Z	E
L			H		N		R
A	N	K	L	E		D	U	E	S
N		I		R		E		S
C	A	N	Y	O	N	S		T

88.
```
 I C E A G E
   A   S M   S
S H R E K   P A Y
T     S   T   D
E L S A   H Y M N
A   I   S     E
D I M   W O O D Y
Y   B     R
   A N T H E M
```

89.
```
P U F F E D     S
O     R   O T T O
N     O   W   O
D R A G O N F L Y
E     N       E
G A R D E N I N G
  P   A   E     L
W E E D   W     U
  R   S E T T L E
```

90.
```
B U S H E S     P
R   L     P E L E
A R A B   E   O
Z   P E N A L T Y
I   C   K     E
L U C K I E R   L
  G   H   R E A L
G L E A M   E   O
  Y   M E A D O W
```

91.
```
B A S I L     P A T
U   E   I   O   H
S U N F L O W E R
  T   Y   E   O
D I E T   G R E W
A   N   P   L
I N C O R R E C T
S   E   O   S   I
Y E S   W A S T E
```

92.
```
B I R D T A B L E
  R   A   U   A
K I L N   N A V Y
  S   D   T   E
    P E A   A N T
  S   L   S   D
H E S I T A T E D
E   O   G   R
D O N K E Y
```

93.
```
W A N D   A R M S
I       E   O   O
D U T C H   W H Y
O       I   L   O
W I N D M I L L S
      E   N   L
D   A D M I R A L
O   G     N   N
C L O G   G O D S
```

94.
```
B E A N S T A L K
A   R   U   N   E
B A K E R   G U Y
Y     P   U   S
  D W A R F S
J   H   I   O
A L I   S E V E N
C   T   E   E   C
K N E A D   T E E
```

95.
```
B I L B O   B I B
F     L   U   R
G A N D A L F   A
  O   F   F   I
T O T O   F A U N
O   I   P   L
P   C R A Y O N S
I   E   T   L
C O D   H A R R Y
```

96.
```
B E L L   K N O B
I   E   T   O   E
R E E K S   B U N
O     H   E   Z
  B R A I L L E
J   A   R     W
O L D   T I A R A
B   I   S   W   T
S N O T   B E N T
```

97.
```
P I N G P O N G
  C   O   A L
H E A L   R A I N
  H   F   S   D
H O P       T E N
  C   W   E
S K I I N G   L
  E   L   G E A R
C Y C L E S   P
```

98.
```
E I G H T Y   H
I     A   O V E N
G   R U G   R
H A T E   A T E
T   E     W   F
  O N E   S O L O
  M   V A T   R
F I V E   U   T
T   N I N E T Y
```

99.
```
N A T U R A L   A
    R   U   O R B
B R A N S O N   B
I   F   K   D   A
G L A D   B O W
B   L   C   N   G
E   G A L L E R Y
N   A   A   Y   M
  P R I N C E S S
```

100.
```
  C A N A R Y
S   A   A   U
H E N   S I E V E
O   O   A   A
W R E N   E G G S
E   K   O   I
R A V E N   O W L
  A   E   S   Y
  S N E E Z E
```

101.
```
P I C N I C   B
A   O   H E A P  P
C H O I C E   K
K   K   A F T E R
  T   V     R
N U R S E   K   S
  T   A R T I S T
P O E M     L   A
  R   E D I T O R
```

102.
```
  P A C I F I C
H   N   R   N G
E X T R A   D O E
L   Q   I   R
P E R U   W A R M
F   E   U     A
U S A   S P A I N
L   L   S   R   Y
  E M B R A C E
```

103

```
G O B L I N S   L
R     I     M O O
O     M     I   G
W E R E W O L F
L   I   H   E   A
  S P O O K Y   T
  E   G   I S N T
F E A R L     I
  K   E X O T I C
```

104

```
A L P H A B E T
  E   A   O   O
F O O L   R O O F
O     L U G   L
L O G O     L O U
D     W   A   N
S P I E L B E R G
  O   E   E   A
  P E N E L O P E
```

105

```
  G I R A F F E
B   T   S   U   G
U S E   K E N Y A
F   M   S       Z
F I S H   T R U E
A     B   H   L
L A S S O   I L L
O   P   L   N   E
  W A R T H O G
```

106

```
  M E E R K A T
C   Y   O   W   L
H Y E N A   F E E
E     R   U   O
E G G S   F L A P
T   A   H     A
A P T   E N T E R
H   E   I   I   D
  O S T R I C H
```

107

```
Z I P P E D   E
I     R   O I N K
N     O   T   E
C H E M I S T R Y
  E         G
A L S O   R A Y S
  I   S   U   A
F U E L   N   L
M   O U T F I T
```

108

```
C A L C I U M
H   O     A   N
L   T U R T L E
O U S T   O   O
R   O X Y G E N
I R O N   C
N   K   F E R N S
E   A   A   A   A
  H Y D R O G E N
```

109

```
T A P I R     B
E   R   O F T E N
A   O   O     G
M A D   T W I G S
  M         E
  A N A C O N D A
  Z   U   E   R
M O I S T   R   C
N     S L O T H
```

110

```
E L E C T R I C
E   G   R     R
L A   P O I S O N
  J   P     C
T R A G I C   O
U   G   C   A D S
T O U C A N   I
U   A   L A D L E
S U R F   G   E
```

111

```
  M O N S O O N
    I   H   A   G
D E L H I   T E A
E     N       N
B O L L Y W O O D
A   A     U   H
T E N   H A N   I
E   K   U   C
  M A N G O E S
```

112

```
W H I R L W I N D
A   R     E   O
S N O W S T O R M
P   N
  M I S P L A C E
F   N   E   G   I
L I G H T N I N G
E     A   L   H
E X C E L L E N T
```

113

```
  D A N U B E
G U   I   E
A I M   L O D G E
N   B   E     N
G L O W   T O A D
E     P   C   U
S E I N E   E A R
    C   T   A   E
  S E V E R N
```

114

```
M O N A L I S A
A   I   E   A
G   P H A N T O M
I     V     N
C R E P E   H I T
  O   R   C   O
J U D O   A N N A
  G   O   F   R
  E I F F E L   C
```

115

```
B R O A D W A Y
I   P   R     A
G E T   O P E N S
A       O     K
P   E M P I R E
P   M     H E Y
L I B E R T Y   A
E   E   O   M O W
  B R I D G E   N
```

116

```
P E N C I L   T
L   L   E C H O
A R E A   X   O
N     R U L E R S
E     K   U   H
T I C K E T   I
R   E   H I V E
S O O N   O   L
N   T H R E A D
```

117

```
  S E R P E N T S
C   A   O   E   O
R O T   L E W I S
E   E   O   W
W I N D   C O O K
  V   R   R   N
  O   A P O L L O
T R E K   A D   T
Y   E   F     S
```

118

```
H O L L Y     A S H
A   E   U   I     O
G U M   O K   C E D A R S
P I N E   C O N E
A       S   L
L O F T Y   I D O
M     I   N   V   W
S I R   C R E T E
```

119

```
S P O N G E       T
O     A   A C R E X
L I M P E T   C A T E
D     A   S N A I L
C U T   C   A     S
R     H E R M I T
A     U   I
B A I T   O I L Y
```

120

```
S E A W E E D       B
T   D   A   I     A
A N D   S P E A R R N
R   E   T       N
F U R Y   L A V A C
I       F   L   L
S U S H I   I L L E
H   O   R   G   E
  A N E M O N E S
```

121

```
P O O D L E     S
I     E   D O C K
E     A   G     R
R E T R I E V E R
  U       E     E
G R E Y H O U N D
  O   E   D     A
O P A L   D     N
  E   L A S S I E
```

122

```
  C H A R L E S
G   U   E
R U S S E L L   G
O   K   L   E   G
M A Y O   S T A R
I       S   T   M
T A R A N T U L A
M       A   C   N
P U P P I E S
```

123

```
  P E A C O C K S
T   M   O   A   O
A K A   C A R O L
D   I   K   P   A
P O L A R B E A R
O       O   N
L I B R A   T O P
E   E   C   E   I
  S E A H O R S E
```

124

```
Z E R O   Z O N E
U   A     Z     G
L A Z Y   D O Z Y
U   O   A   N   P
  C R A Z I E S T
J       T       E
A M A Z E   Z A G
Z   C   C   O   U
Z I T S   Z O O M
```

First published in 2016 by Usborne Publishing Ltd, 83–85 Saffron Hill, London ECIN 8RT, England.
Copyright © 2016 Usborne Publishing Ltd. The name Usborne and the devices ♕ ⊕ are Trade Marks of Usborne Publishing Ltd.